GREAT MOMENTS IN
F O O T B A L L

Interviews, Quotes, Wisdom, and
Inspiration from Past & Present
Professional and Collegiate Coaches

The Halftime Book Project

Randy Walker, Northwestern University Football
Dick Jauron, Buffalo Bills
Don Grossnickle –Project Coordinator/Editor

ISBN: 0-9787788-7-1

Library of Congress: 2006934923

First Edition

All Rights Reserved
Printed in the United States

Cover art and design: Jen Nebel
Incite Studio, Ltd. 735 S. Evergreen Ave.
Arlington Heights, IL 60005 847-577-0518

Printed in the United States

CONTACT AND DONATION INFORMATION
Donations to the Halftime Book Project may be made payable to:
Halftime Book Project Ltd*
C/O Dreams for Kids
155 N. Michigan, Suite 700
Chicago, IL 60601
Toll-free at 1-866-729-5454

Note: *The Halftime Book Project is not yet a 501 (c) (3) charity

The Halftime Book Project Ltd and Dreams for Kids have worked together on behalf of Rob Komosa and Rocky Clark. It is hoped that a portion of the net proceeds might benefit the excellent work of Dreams for Kids.

Donations for Dreams for Kids can be made payable to: Dreams for Kids:
155 N. Michigan, Suite 700
Chicago, IL 60601 Donation information (312) 729-5405.
Toll-free at 1-866-729-5454

Dreams for Kids is a registered non-profit 501(c)(3) charity which provides assistance to improve the quality of life for children with disabilities and those who have suffered hardship. Dreams for Kids offer education, recreation, financial assistance and hope to children through various programs.

Dreams for Kids

CONTENTS

Great Moments in Football Halftime

Interviews, Quotes, Wisdom, and Inspiration from Past & Present Professional and Collegiate Coaches

ACKNOWLEDGMENTS

This project has come to completion through the persistent contributions of many individuals.

Special thanks go to Rob Komosa and Rocky Clark and families. Their courageous spirit in the face of adversity is a beautiful gift to all. Special thanks go to Randy Walker, coach friend, advocate. Coach Walker and Dick Jauron provided the initial leadership and made the invitations to colleagues. Thanks to Jamie Walker for the inspirational foreword and to the entire Walker family for loyal support. Thanks to all the coaches who have shared their quotes, stories, insights, anecdotes, and interviews. They were not too busy to take time and support the boys.

Thanks to John Bostrom, Senior Director of Administration, Caroline Guip, Director of Community Relations for the Chicago Bears. They have been key figures in supporting all aspects of this project.

Thanks to Jen Nebel and Incite Studio in Arlington Heights for the artwork for the invitation packets sent out to the coaches and the book cover design. Thanks to Tim Green and Warner Books for the inside look of the NFL locker room from a player's perspective. Thanks to NFL.com and Vic Carucci for permission to include the fantastic article about Superbowl Halftime.

Thanks to Kim Duchossois for faithful love and financial support for the project. Thanks to Erin Holmes, Jim Stapleton, Elena Valenzuela, and Gerry Souter for technical assistance with the manuscript.

Thanks to project supporters: Tom and Ann Paine, Brian and Joanna Metzger, John and Connie Griffin, Betsy Wilson, Bob and Judy Anderson, Tom Dickey, and Jim and Christine Thomas. Thanks to Jersey's Pizza and Grill, 2360 Lakewood Blvd, Hoffman Estates, IL. 60195

Thanks to Marilyn Foster Publisher of Lumen-Us Publications for her dedicated professionalism and strong commitment to a quality product. Thanks to Tom Tuohy and the Dreams for Kids organization for loyal encouragement.

Thanks to the Kathy Grossnickle and family, for unwavering love, sacrifices and support in guiding the project through to completion. I never could have made it without their inspiration.

WITH APPRECIATION TO THE CONTRIBUTING HALFTIME BOOK PROJECT PARTICIPANTS

Randy Walker –Northwestern University (In Memoriam)
Dick Jauron- Coach Buffalo Bills-Former Coach Chicago Bears
Lovie Smith-Coach Chicago Bears
Art Shell-Coach Oakland Raiders
Tommy West-Coach University of Memphis
Tim Green-Former Player, Atlanta Falcons
Vic Carucci-Sportswriter, NFL.com
Jamie Walker-Asst Director of Football Operations
Northwestern University
Terry Hoeppner – Coach Indiana University
Greg Schiano – Coach Rutgers University
Dan Reeves – Former Coach Atlanta Falcons
Kirk Ferentz – Coach University of Iowa
Mike Martz – Asst Coach-Detroit Lions
Urban Meyer – Coach University of Florida
Ken Hatfield – Former Coach, Rice University
Jim Tressel-Coach The Ohio State University
Andy McCollum-Former Coach Middle Tennessee State
Ron Turner-Asst Coach Chicago Bears
Bobby Bowden Coach Florida State University
Fisher Deberry-Coach Air Force Academy
Dave Wannstedt- Coach University of Pittsburgh,
David Cutliffe-Asst Coach University of Tennessee
Nick Saban-Coach Miami Dolphins
John Machovic-Former Coach University of Arizona
Mike Ditka-Former Coach Chicago Bears, New Orleans Saints
Gary Barnett-Former Coach University of Colorado
Bob Stoops-Coach University of Oklahoma
Dom Capers-Asst Coach Miami Dolphins
Andy Reid-Coach Philadelphia Eagles

Tom Coughlin-Coach New York Giants

Mark Richt-Coach University of Georgia

Brian Billick-Coach Baltimore Ravens

Paul Pasqualoni-Asst Coach Dallas Cowboys

Jim Hofher-Former Coach University of Buffalo

Frank Solich-Coach Ohio University

Ron Zook-Coach University of Illinois

Paul Johnson-Coach Naval Academy

Frank Beamer-Coach Virginia Tech

Lloyd Carr-Coach University of Michigan

Bill Cowher-Coach Pittsburgh Steelers

Bob Pruett- Former Coach Marshall University

Al Groh- Coach University of Virginia

Barry Alvarez-Former Coach University of Wisconsin

Pat Fitzgerald, Coach Northwestern University

PREFACE

First, thank you for purchasing this book. Your financial support helps two paralyzed former high school football athletes obtain the services, housing, and equipment needed to enhance the quality of their lives. With a portion of the proceeds we hope to establish a foundation that could support future high school football athletes who suffer catastrophic injuries.

The football family has rallied to encourage and support Rocky Clark and Rob Komosa. Not looking the other way and sweeping the realities and needs of these two quadriplegic young men under the carpet takes guts. In solidarity we send a message to them that people care. Their struggle is often lonely and painful. They do their best each day to rebuild their lives after a devastating and catastrophic spinal cord injury suddenly changed everything.

This book takes an intensive look inside the college and professional football locker room at halftime. It is a rare "fly-on-the-wall" peek into the 'other' halftime show. It portrays the often dramatic and intense unleashing of motivation, inspiration, passion and strategizing, played out in the crucible and heat of the inner sanctum of the locker room.

It is said in football, sports, and life:

"When the going gets *tough*, the *tough* get going."

Halftime in football presents an opportunity for the "*tough*" to get into high gear and find strength of character.

Halftime is set aside for the preparation of tough-minded players and coaches to regroup and set into motion a second half strategic game plan that can lead to victory. Little is known about what really goes on between coaches and players inside the college and professional football locker room at halftime. A code of secrecy often prevails, often for good reason.

Many coaches describe football with all its mental toughness along with physical demands as a "microcosm" of life itself. Legendary coach Lou Holtz speaks about what he sees as a close inter-connection between football, coaching and life:

> *"I don't coach football, I coach life. I try to draw analogies between what happens in football and what will happen in life. I try to prepare players for success."*

The Halftime Book Project was initiated in late 2002 as a means to financially benefit two Chicago-area high school football players who have fallen on tough times. Rob Komosa and Rocky Clark became quadriplegic, requiring mechanical breathing assistance. Rob was injured in 1999 and, Rocky in 2000. The boys and their families continue to face tough challenges of many kinds. Coach Randy Walker and Coach Dick Jauron observed the plight of Rocky and Rob and decided to mobilize the nationwide football coaching family to come to their assistance.

On New Year's Day 2003, over 300 invitation letters and packets were assembled by my family and later mailed to NFL and Division 1 college coaches. The packets described the launch of the "Halftime Book Project." Jauron and Walker reached out to their colleagues requesting that they share great moments and perspectives about football halftime. The idea was to compile an intense look into the locker room at halftime. The response from the coaches was excellent. Copies of the project invitation letter sent to the coaches and 'idea generator" are included as the book appendices.

As project coordinator my main role was to weave the contributions from the coaches, and gather research and other sources to help the reader achieve a glimpse into halftime dynamics. I was fortunate to conduct the interviews graciously given by the participating coaches. I had the pleasure of relaying to Rocky and Rob news and messages from each participating coach that stepped forward to help with the project. The final product here is a work in progress, and a labor of love. I will be the first to admit that I am not a professional sportswriter. The best I can say about my credentials as the project editor is that one of my younger brothers was an outstanding all-state high school football player, and later played at the college level. Rob and Rocky are my great friends and they have inspired me by their courage and resilience

The most important message we can all send to Rob and Rocky is that they are not forgotten. In a sense, they are in a halftime period of their lives. In the first half they could run and move on their own. Today, they are rebuilding and adjusting to their paralysis. Our hope for the boys is, 'that when the going gets tough,' they do not give up hope. It is our prayer that they continue pursuing the second half of their lives with spirit, optimism, character and passion.

Don Grossnickle
Project Coordinator

DEDICATION

**COACH
RANDY
WALKER
1954-2006**

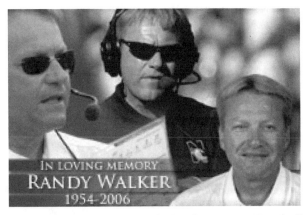

Photo Courtesy of Northwestern Football

This book is dedicated to the memory of Northwestern University Football Coach Randy Walker who died suddenly on June 29, 2006.

It was Coach Walker's desire to pursue this book as a way to support Rob Komosa and Rasul (Rocky) Clark. Coach Walker provided important leadership, motivation and supplied bottomless inspiration for this book project. Randy Walker possessed the fortitude to confront the realities and impact of the spinal cord injuries and did his best to help. Randy and Dick Jauron were responsible for personally inviting fellow coaches from the college and NFL ranks to lock arms as a football family and seek a way to support the boys. Randy made it his business to insure that these injured players would not become lost and neglected. Coach Walker sought ways to bring out the best in Rob and Rocky. Coach Walker was a powerful role model and motivator. He loved being a coach on and off of the field, and it showed.

Coach Walker was a tireless advocate for Rocky and Rob. Randy Walker's spirit remains tenderly in our hearts. We will never forget him!

FOREWORD

My dad spoke a lot about attitude. Whether he was coaching the 12-year-olds on my little league team, the 20-year-olds on his football teams, or speaking to a group of middle-aged alums, it was often about attitude.

He would say that everyone always has a choice. You can choose to have the right attitude, or you can choose to have the wrong attitude. In our family, and with my father's teams, the only real choice was to have a positive attitude.

I ran up to my father after we beat Ohio State in 2004. Obviously, he was ecstatic, but it is easy to be positive after a big win. He said to me, "That was pretty good, wasn't it?" Of course it was a great feeling, and when something that positive happens in your life, it is easy to keep a positive attitude.

However, my Uncle Rob recently reminded me of a conversation he had with my father shortly after our game against Penn State in 2002. It was the Sunday after we had just been shut-out by the Nittany Lions, 49-0, in Beaver Stadium. This game was viewed by the coaching staff as a turning point, good or bad, for the Northwestern Football Program. We had come off a heartbreaking 2001 season and the 2002 campaign was not looking any brighter.

In the locker room after the game, my dad said to his players, "This is a program that is at the verge of doing some great things, and achieving some milestones that have never occurred in the history of Northwestern football. We have had to deal with too many disappointments this year, and we can either keep taking it, or we can do something about it."

In any case, in remembering that following Sunday, my uncle remembered asking my father, "How is the team doing?" My father replied by saying he was interested in seeing how the players would respond, how the coaches would respond, and if the team could figure out a way to move forward.

My uncle then asked, "Okay, but how are you doing?" My father replied in his well-known southern Ohio drawl, "I'm doin' great!" He did not hesitate. He did not skirt around anything. He simply said how he felt. The fact was, he was always "doin' great" because nothing was going to shake him from staying positive.

The best halftime speeches are not kitschy or gimmicky; they do not berate the players or insult the other team; and they are not a forum for coaches to "go off" on any players that made mistakes in the first half. The best halftime speeches (or post-game speeches) remind players to keep a positive attitude, and remind them to continue moving forward, no matter how hard it seems.

Granted, staying positive is not always easy, and it was a lot easier when my dad was around to say, "I'm doin' great!" After his passing, the things he said, the lessons he taught, and his memorable quotes have been comforting, but I am still going to miss my best friend. Difficult times are not easy, but I know my father would have told me to, "keep a positive attitude, and keep moving forward and good things will start to happen."

I hope that the speeches, writings, and thoughts in this book can help you stay positive, whether life is "shutting you out," or you just "beat Ohio State in double-overtime."

Jamie Walker, Son of
Northwestern and Miami
University Head Coach
Randy Walker (1954 – 2006)

"Any man's finest hour, the greatest fulfillment of all that he holds dear, is that moment when he has worked his heart out for a good cause and lies exhausted on the field of battle—victorious."

Vince Lombardi

INTRODUCTION

Dick Jauron, Head Coach of the Buffalo Bills
Former Head Coach Chicago Bears

It is an honor for me to help set the stage for this book; this project is very meaningful to me for many reasons. For starters, I have come to believe that halftime in football is extremely important. More than 50 of my fellow coaches and I have put our heads together toward giving readers an inside look into the inner sanctum of the football locker room. We have undertaken the "Halftime Project" as a way to support two young football players from the Chicago area: Rocky Clark and Rob Komosa. Both of these young men were paralyzed while playing the game for which we all share a love and a passion.

I have come to be inspired by the courage and determination of these boys and their families, who have had to overcome incredibly difficult circumstances. I am very impressed and proud that the football community is rallying to support them during a time that both boys call the "halftime of their lives."

As persons with quadriplegia, Rob and Rocky no longer can pursue life in the same way they once did. Things are different now; they have bravely faced this fact. I am fortunate, to have witnessed their exemplary attitudes. I have been impressed with the attitude and motivation they have demonstrated in rising to the challenges that they face each day of their lives.

In the last several years, I have had conversations with them and shared powerful dialogue that convinces me of a mutual commitment to live our lives according to a game plan built on motivation. Rob and Rocky – and, in fact, all of us – have contributions to make with our lives. I truly believe that. As a coach, that is my passion: to nurture, support, teach and bring out the best in every member of our football family.

For now, I'd like to commend Rob, Rocky and their families for the manner in which they have overcome struggles and pursued every option for the continued improvement of their status. I know they will continue that process with faith in the future. They have seen the results of hard work. They have hard work in front of them.

Their development is critically important. They need to keep working physically. And they need to keep working mentally, emotionally and intellectually. For the time being, their ability to express themselves with movement has been shut down. What remains is an opportunity to pursue the intellectual side of things – to develop their minds through all kinds of different strategies to come out victorious. I feel very strongly that all people can keep striving for improvement and have that great strength, great hope and great faith to know that good things will come in time.

Rocky, Coach Dick Jauron and Rob at
Halas Hall, the Chicago Bears
Training Facility in
Lake Forest Illinois

Barry Alvarez
Athletic Director, Former Head Coach
University of Wisconsin

It is a tremendous honor and privilege to contribute to this project. I am fortunate, and feel blessed, to be working daily in an arena that surrounds me with phenomenal young men who continually inspire me to levels of performance never dreamed of. Rob Komosa and Rocky Clark are two young men that face life and all of its uncertainties with passionate purpose, prideful persistence, uncommon poise, fierce determination, compelling conviction and – most importantly – infectious enthusiasm.

As a head football coach, I believe a positive attitude and commitment to excellence are indispensable qualities for success. Rob and Rocky are two young men who live these qualities vigorously and optimally. Celebrated civil rights leader, Dr. Martin Luther King, once said, "You have to give yourself entirely."

Then once you make up your mind that you are giving yourself, you are prepared to do anything that serves that cause and advances the movement. I have reached that point I have given myself fully."

Rob and Rocky have certainly given themselves fully, and I know they will continue to give more than they receive. I can only hope that they will continue to fight on through the traffic in their life and pave new roads for others to follow.

What an inspiration they both truly are! I'd like to share my two favorite pieces of written inspiration: quotations from Charles Swindoll, and former president Theodore Roosevelt.

Attitude
Charles Swindoll

"The longer I live, the more I realize the impact of attitude on life.

Attitude, to me, is more important than facts. It is more important than the past, than education, than money, than circumstances, than failures, than successes, than what other people think or say or do. It is more important than appearance, giftedness, or skill. It will make or break a company ... a church ... a home. The remarkable thing is we have a choice every day regarding the attitude we will embrace for that day. We cannot change the inevitable. The only thing we can do is play on the one string we have, and that is our attitude ... I am convinced that life is 10% what happens to me, and 90% how I react to it. And so it is with you ... we are in charge of our Attitudes."

The Man in the Arena
Theodore Roosevelt

"It is not the critic who counts; not the man who points out how the strong man stumbles, or where the doer of deeds could have done them better.

The credit belongs to the man who is actually in the arena, whose face is marred by dust and sweat and blood; who strives valiantly; who errs, who comes short again and again, because there is no effort without error and shortcoming; but who does actually strive to do the deeds; who knows great enthusiasms, the great devotions; who spends himself in a worthy cause; who at the best knows in the end the triumph of high achievement, and who at the worst, if he fails, at least fails while daring greatly, so that his place shall never be with those cold and timid souls who neither know victory nor defeat."

"When one door of happiness closes, another opens; but often we look so long at the closed door that we do not see the one which has opened for us."

Helen Keller

Meet Rob and Rocky

Robert (Rob) Komosa   *Rasul (Rocky) Clark*

The following is a combined re-creation of the events that led to the injury of these players.

Imagine it is now……..October 6, 1999, or September 16, 2000

Imagine the scene of football fields………..

Rob Komosa is playing in an after school football practice, while Rocky Clark is participating in an official game.

Action…………………………………..Rocky is poised behind the offensive line ready to receive and carry the ball. Rob is poised and ready to do the same………………………..

The quarterback barks out the play with signals like these:

…..Ready, set, blue 24 ISO, hut, hut,-

The quarterback hands off the ball. At the line of scrimmage there is a crash of shoulder pads and grunts uttered. On the line of scrimmage is a tangle of human bodies and physical energy. Rob and Rocky are the ball carriers. They make a dash for daylight. Off they go, 5 yards, ten and more. The exhilaration is intoxicating. The running backs break loose.

Suddenly, the impact of tackling defenders interrupts the running rhythm and trips their feet. An unsettling sensation of loss of control halts the excitement and in its place emerges an uneasy sense of panic and fear. Off balance, there arises an uncomfortable feeling of falling and disequilibrium signaling an increasing loss of control. The mind subconsciously reviews the message pounded into their heads by coach, "no matter what, you must tuck that ball in and hold on, to the point of collision with that hard unbending ground." You must concentrate and hold onto the ball. There must be no fumble.

Inside the ball carrier's brain a horrible sensation erupts. Bang, and in another instant black, followed by a flash of light in the brain, and then nothing.

And then nothing…….. And then nothing…………

The injured players lose consciousness. They lie face down motionless as hundreds of pounds of adolescent energy and sinew peel slowly off of them. In perhaps 5 to 10 seconds, players and coaches come to the realization and horror that the ball carriers are motionless, strangely still.

The coaches and players rivet their eyes and attention to look for some very welcome sign of movement. The injured player's body remains still, limp, and lifeless. The prolonged moment of stillness reveals the makings of a crisis. "He isn't breathing" somebody yells in a panic. "Get some help" The coaches rush to their player's side. The trainer arrives and sees the body wreckage and quickly confirms that there is no breathing, no sign of life. Somebody yells in a panicked voice,

"Call 9-11" Efforts to revive prove unsatisfactory. CPR is begun.

The teammates stand silent in shock and anticipation. They desperately want to be assured that their teammate would be OK. One says to the other in disbelief, "just an instant ago he was fine." A buzz goes forward by everybody gawking at the bizarre scene as players ask each other, "What happened?" The emergency vehicle hastily leaves the field. Now the waiting begins, so many anticipate hearing any news about the injured player's status. Silently the witnesses wonder, "Did he make it, will he be alright?"

Rumor begins to spread that it appears to be a catastrophic spine injury. The mention of possible residual paralysis begins to surface. In the aftermath, stories are told that Komosa's head and helmet were crushed as a loud crash followed a collision with a concrete and metal fence post looming on the gridiron sideline. Clark's situation was a neck and spine twisted and snapped under the weight of tacklers. Komosa's injury happened at suburban Rolling Meadows High School (IL) during after school practice on October 6, 1999. Rocky's injury took place during a game he was playing at south suburb, Eisenhower High School in Blue Island (IL) on September 16, 2000 when Rocky's team was playing Oak Forest High School.

Rocky and Rob do not recall anything beyond the crack of the tackles. They were apparently immediately unconscious and unaware of emergency personnel performing CPR. Physicians later mentioned being astounded that the boys survived, as most persons who sustain this depth of injury die within moments. Both boys found their way to the Northwestern Memorial Hospital and later moved to the Spinal

Cord Rehabilitation Center in Chicago. (Rehabilitation Institute of Chicago) Both boys were fitted with a metal "halo" apparatus that immobilizes the head and neck so that it can heal. The metal halo is a frame which is positioned on the outside of the head and grotesquely secured by painfully screwing in points into the flesh and skull of the head.

Rob and Rocky recall their first waking in the hospital and being in a daze. They slowly came to comprehend their horrible status. They recall times where they cried in disbelief. They soon came to recognize that life as they knew it was now behind them. They found themselves thrown into a dark cavern of horror, a nightmare that would not go away. Komosa asked for headphones to listen to the chaotic heavy metal rock band, Mettalica. Mettalica's song title, "Trapped Under the Ice" provided a realistic picture of Rob's perceived status. At times, dark moments of incomparable sadness, despair and depression overtook the boys and their families.

Rob first met Rocky as he was summoned to the rehab hospital responding to a call to visit and cheer up Rocky whose spirits had become dangerously low. Rocky was severely depressed at the time. A friendship was struck and continues today. Their faith somehow carried the day. Encouragement from family, friends and the football family meant a great deal. Rehabilitation and adjustment to fully quadriplegic bodies and breathing assisted by a mechanical ventilator was slow and grueling. The boys returned to their respective homes several long months after their injury. Periods of loneliness and despair were frequent once they returned home. Outreach and encouragement by a few friends and new friends from the community provided doses of hope and optimism. The financial consequences evident in the aftermath of the crisis added much to their pain. The injury changed so much. Their home environment resembled a clinic or hospice arrangement with all of the equipment filling up the small space. Each required twenty four hour care in order to attend to their new routines. Bladder and bowel functions became involuntary. The boys needed to be fed their food. Annette Clark and Barbara Komosa the boys mothers each were forced to quit their jobs in order to care for them. This situation placed the family finances into a crashing tailspin. There was no alternative. In time, both boys returned to finish their high school diplomas. Rocky is attending a local community college making an effort to pursue some classes. His health and problems with transportation make regular attendance difficult.

Rocky Clark and halo apparatus

Rob Komosa and halo apparatus

ROB AND ROCKY'S HALFTIME MESSAGE

Robert (Rob) Komosa   *Rasul (Rocky) Clark*

The halftime periods of our lives have been a roller coaster. In the first half, we were both walking and running, and playing football. Considering the events of late, we definitely needed a new game plan. Halftime means a great deal to us. The coaches and the people that have stood by us as we roll our wheelchairs forward helping us make a new game plan are wonderful. These coaches along with friends, have sparked positive feelings that mysteriously represent a force that drives us forward. We have confidence in our coaches and listen to their direction. However, one of the most profound insights that we have gained is that despite the support that comes from others, our destiny is *ours,* and we must be the ones to activate it.

A favorite quote comes from Helen Keller: "When one door of happiness closes, another opens; but often we look so long at the closed door that we do not see the one which has opened for us." To be really honest, it seems as if, a big powerful door in our lives suddenly slammed closed right in our faces knocking us down. Fact is, we haven't the means yet to get back up on our own. We seek the open door. We are in the process of pulling ourselves together and doing our best to look optimistically for the open doors ahead of us.

To say that we are struggling is an understatement. Not only are we struggling, but these paralyzing injuries have brought havoc to our families. We have become more than 24 hour a day full time jobs for our mothers who must play the role of our constant caregivers to keep us alive. We are at a time of our lives when most every other guy our age is working on his own independence and separating himself from parents and his childhood home. We are far from being ready to do that. To see the pain and anguish of what our injuries have brought to our families is almost worse than being frozen in paralyzed bodies that refuse to respond to our most simple commands. Yet, we do not lose hope.

The support the coaches have offered has provided many rays of sunshine we feel on our faces. It is a fact that our faces are the only part of our bodies that we now can genuinely feel. The warmth and kindness of their outreach means so much. The struggles we face are difficult. The agony, confusion, anger, and self pity seem to give way when good news comes. The isolation we feel is tremendous. We are physically cut off from feeling any senses with our bodies. We are not only trapped inside of our bodies, but have no means to move and escape to anywhere.

Our "open door," as Helen Keller describes it, has to be our mind, our attitude, our motivation, our spirit, our faith. These intangibles are the fuel that keeps us going. These same emotional factors are what football coaches and players utilize to drive them onward. Football is a game we both still love very much. Playing the sport resulted in us getting much more than we ever realized and were bargaining for. However, we understand that looking back isn't productive. What's done is done. Just like a football game. The score at halftime cannot be changed. The score is a fact. When a football contest is completed and the time runs out, the results remain only as a matter for the record books. Regrets are non-productive. You could say that the first half of our lives is also now history. Things cannot be change even though with all of our hearts, we wish we cannot turn back time. We cannot create a different circumstance and reverse that moment when fate seemed to play a cruel and mean trick on us, tackling us hard, so hard we could never get up.

Many people often give us advice, and try to cheer us up. We realize they mean well. The coaches that have called and written making contributions to this book have motivated us, impressed us, and convinced us that there are people who do care. It is very easy to lay back and feel the tears well up getting emotional about our predicament. Sadly, each year, according to national statistics, about ten high school athletes will endure head, neck and spinal cord injuries. A few will die. The athletes and their families must find their own personal way to deal with things, confront the "closed doors" Helen Keller speaks about in her inspiring writings.

We find that in the process of getting used to our condition there are good days and bad. We must courageously face dark moments. We choose to measure progress in very small increments. The best kind of day we can have is one where we find optimism and hope. With those positive emotions going for us, we know, no matter what, it will be a good day. We realize that if we wallow in our self pity we will go no further. If we wallow, we travel only to ugly despair, despondency, depression and even to the place where we wonder if we want to live. We get into deep depression and can only see dark pathways ahead as we lay motionless watching the world passing us by.

We have been to dark places of broken spirit. Some people have even asked us if we every have the thought of wishing that we would have just died instead of recovering like this. No, we tell them. We are optimistic. We imagine that there must be a mysterious reason to explain why we did not die. We still search for an explanation for why we were spared. We seek the wisdom to find a way to use our lives for a positive purpose. We have been paralyzed now for a period of several years. So much has happened, many tears, and many cheers.

Travis Roy, a hockey player, endured a paralyzing incident during the first 11 seconds of his college hockey career at Boston College. We look to him and other paralyzed athletes as role models to help us deal with our current circumstance. We hope that there are progressive pathways ahead that we can enter that lead to us out of helplessness. Travis Roy writes: "We must continue to chart a course for our lives. We must set goals and live every day to the fullest as we strive to achieve them. If life takes an unexpected turn, hang on to the goals that are still realistic, and reassess those that are not. Our value systems remain unchanged. It is these core values that provide the foundation for setting a new course. That course may lead us in directions that we never anticipated, or even dreamed of. But that new course may lead us to making contributions and accomplishments that are of more value to society than those we had originally planned for ourselves."

We both look for inspiration every day as a way to not focus on the past but, rather have hope, obtain optimism and inspiration. Below is a meaningful poem that was given to us by Tom Tuohy, President of the Chicago Dreams for Kids. We believe that it speaks a powerful message. We can imagine that a coach might read it at halftime as a pep talk.

William Ernest Henley. 1849–1903
Invictus

Out of the night that covers me,
Black as the Pit from pole to pole,
I thank whatever gods may be
For my unconquerable soul.
In the fell clutch of circumstance
I have not winced nor cried aloud.
Under the bludgeonings of chance
My head is bloody, but unbowed.

Beyond this place of wrath and tears
Looms but the Horror of the shade,
And yet the menace of the years
Finds, and shall find, me unafraid.

It matters not how strait the gate,
How charged with punishments the scroll,
I am the master of my fate:
I am the captain of my soul

In closing of our message to the reader, we offer our heartfelt hope and prayer that we can somehow continue to find courage each and every day of the second half of our lives. We pledge to do our best to stubbornly travel forward embracing the gift of life and sharing ourselves and our journey with others. We still love football. Halftime matters.

R.K. R.C.

Rocky and Rob Interviewing the Legendary Coach "Iron" Mike Ditka at Ditka's Restaurant in Chicago-January 2005

"Coaches who can outline plays on a blackboard are a dime a dozen. The ones who win get inside their players and motivate."

Vince Lombardi

1

Locker Room Halftime:
The "Look and Feel"

Tick, tick tick…The essence of football is played out as a race against limited time. The final seconds on the clock on the scoreboard wind down as the players complete the final play of the half. The horn sounds and the assembled crowd let out a roar for their team. The scene out on the playing field area is a beehive of activity: The injured players, hobbling on crutches staged along the sideline begin the halftime parade to the locker room getting a head start. Trainers and team members

not on the field, soon follow them. The players participating in the final play ceremoniously trot off demonstrating an image of conviction and work hard not to not show a shortage of energy. Typically last off the playing field are the coaches and officials.

Typical Pro Locker Room Scene at Halftime-
Houston Texans Locker Room

The locker room door swings open, the sound of the cleats on the tile or cement resonates a clackety clack. Players file in and move toward their respective places for their well earned halftime R and R. Depending upon the score, the emotions and mood reflect the status of the team's progress and how the game is going. 50 to -100 brawny bodies cramp tightly into a confined space. The sights and sounds and smells of sweating bodies evoke a familiar scene. Most of the players have been in this situation many times before and have expectations for their version of the routine. The locker room offers a secluded sanctuary. The brotherhood of secrecy is often sealed when the door is slammed shut and a guard is stationed outside to limit the entrance of any unwelcome intruder. As the halftime drama unfolds the heavy breathing of the players subsides. Helmets are off, and sweat freely rolls down the faces. Some players make their way to a urinal or a stall. Some reach for Gatorade or water to quench their thirst and replace lost body fluids.

Over in a corner, the coaches typically huddle up before they disperse and connect with their designated assemblages. The players wait and anticipate new orders and directions, praise, motivation, or an ass chewing, or criticism and redirection. Honest, sometimes brutally harsh assessments and analysis about team and individual performances come forth. The facial expression and body language of the coaches is perceptively registered and decoded by the players. They read and see a picture of the coach, and a tone for their meeting is set. The players are often crouched against walls, as the limited seating on chairs and benches is at a premium. Support from any wall, locker or floor feels good. Muscle cramps torture many players. For a few moments the rhythm and the pace of the first half of the game changes in the safety of the team's locker room.

The noise of the crowd, the clashing sound of pad against pad and the grunts coming from piles of tacklers gives way to a few moments of relative silence. As the smaller group meetings conclude, the head coach may make his way around the room. As the time grows short until the exodus back onto the field the head coach appears reflective and is busy sizing things up. Football tradition now dictates that all eyes will center on the direction of the location of the head coach. The coach performs according to his own script and carries out his own halftime show. Sometimes the head coach enumerates the tasks ahead. The coach uses his imagination blended with just the right portion of emotion, as he formulates the architecture for the second half battle. The final task of the head coach is to decide how he wishes to communicate the revised plans to his assistants and his team. Typically he will utter some choice words that are intended to have an impact directing his loyal followers. This is a defining moment of truth. The coach must muster any leverage he has to catapult the attitude and confidence in order to somehow guide the momentum forward. Whatever is said must ideally get the second half off to a great start. His communication should help the team as a whole gain the upper hand, stir every individual heart and mind with conviction and store up passion for their common cause. The message and the moment must reverberate until the final seconds remaining in the actual game are gone.

The players will return to this locker room after their appointment with destiny is completed. With bruises and charley horse cramps aching, it is seldom easy to stand up again, stretch out, and prepare for the grand entrance, unless that is, the team is triumphantly returning to the field with a hefty lead and the outcome of the game seems well in hand. There is an extra snap of confidence and swagger in the step when a team returns to the field following halftime.

Unknown opportunities will appear. Mistakes will be made. Big gains will be made, and losses sustained. Injuries will arise. Surprises will dot the panorama. Hopefully, the teamwork and preparation of hundreds of hours of practice and often years of experience will positively pay off and things will go well for the team.

The official's knock is heard on the locker room door and it flies open. The parade begins as thousands of pounds of muscle and sinew emerges rallying out of the locker room showing conviction, resolve, dedication and motivation to do whatever it takes for victory.

* * *

Halftime Training Begins In High School
Locker Rooms Routines

A suburban Chicago high school journalist shares his insights about how emotion grips the high school football locker room. It is here that the seasoned football player learns lessons about what locker room emotion is all about. The article appeared in the Wheeling High School student newspaper in October, 2004. It is written by Jason Wieder.

The lights go out. Everything in the room comes to a complete silence. Thirty-nine high school men gather in a circle still completely silent because they know once they step into the locker room there is no talking and everything is serious from here on out.

"Once I walk into the locker room, I am completely concentrated and focused on the game," Jon Sanchez, junior, said. There is one ball. Tonight this ball represents power. Power that only a few have, power that must be earned, power that comes from the respect of many and represents the pride and tradition of WHS football.

The football player who possesses the ball may talk. Everyone else must listen. Once the person has the ball he may step into the circle and begin to talk. He who possesses the ball now has the attention of all his teammates. For the time he has the ball, he can say whatever he wants to say. This is the way the football players get hyped up and motivated for the upcoming game. Usually only the captains talk, but he who possesses the ball may pass it to whomever he chooses. Tradition says, though, that the person with the ball must have earned the right to talk through either being a captain, a senior, or one who has earned the respect of both. Every Friday night, these locker room talks happen right before the Varsity football team heads out to the field for warm-ups. The talks are intense, they are from the heart, they are nasty, they are vicious, but they represent hard work, determination, courage, will, heart, tears, sweat and all that has been put into the season to that point. "After the captains are finished my heart is pumping and I can't wait to step onto the field," Sanchez, said. Each year these locker room talks have one more tradition. For certain important games, the captains of the Varsity team take these talks to the sophomore level. This adds a little more excitement to their game, to the program, and to underclassmen that perhaps look up to the varsity players. It also teaches them a year early of what to expect in the upcoming year, and teach them of one of the traditions of WHS football. And where else would football players meet before a game other than a dark, hell-like cell. "The room is deathly silent and your entire attention is at the person with the football.

When the captains are finished, you are extremely pumped up and ready to go," Scott Horwitch, senior, said. Once the speeches are given, the circle of players clap, scream and yell until the ball has been passed to the next speaker. Then the silence takes over again. At the end there's one huge, loud mob of angry players yelling HIT, HIT, HIT, HIT, HIT, HIT, HIT, HIT, HIT, HIT, HIT, HIT, HIT, HIT, HIT

* * *

INSIDE A HIGH SCHOOL TEAM LOCKER ROOM: WARE COUNTY GEORGIA

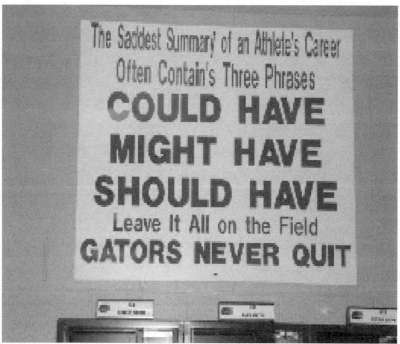

"Knowing is not enough, you must apply. Willing is not enough, you must do."

"Preparation and Execution are the Keys to Victory and Success"

Douglas McArthur

2

Locker Room Views From a Player Perspective

By Tim Green
Former NFL Player- Atlanta Falcons
Best Selling Author
Attorney

What is the locker room really like? Few other than the players and coaches are entitled to enter and see for themselves what occurs here. Among the brotherhood of coaches and players, there exists an explicit and implied code to maintain silence about the locker room goings-on. A photograph from the wall of the Green Bay Packers' locker room proclaims a code of silence: *"What you see here, what you say here, what you hear here, let it stay here … when you leave here."*

In "The Dark Side of the Game," Tim Green, a defensive end for the Atlanta Falcons for eight seasons, tells his story about his life in the professional game. He vividly describes what it really feels like to be a player amid all the hype, fame and fortune. Today, Green is an attorney, a best selling author, and a highly successful commentator for Fox Sports. This is an excerpt from his book titled, From The Dark Side Of The Game: My Life In The NFL by Tim Green © Copyright 1996 by Tim Green. (By permission of Warner Books, Inc).

BEFORE

During the ten minutes before a football game, the anxiety is so incredible that I used to wonder what made people ever want to play the game. Other players share this emotion. If you aren't sick with worry about the impending contest, then you don't care about winning – and if you don't care about winning, you don't wind up playing in the NFL. The pressure to perform well, the pressure to win, the pressure to defeat someone across from you, haunts your every moment during the football season. These tensions mount to a crescendo that reaches sickening proportions just minutes before kickoff. Now is no time for heroic speeches; those are make-believe. Now is the time to purge the bile by vomiting into a pail. This is where the movie image of a player banging his head against a locker comes from. Moments before it's time to go out on the field, the locker room is a mob of jiggling, shaking, cursing, growling men. Their eyes roll like crazed guard dogs throwing themselves against a chain link fence. What they want more than anything is relief, to be set free, to tear the throat out of the thing that torments them.

Out of this horrible set of emotions, the joy of the game is born. In the freedom of that first violent crack of pads, the tension leaves you like a grounded surge of electricity. It is so completely gone that you wonder if it was ever there at all. There is no nervousness, no thought of fear, after that first hit. The butterflies (more like three-foot fruit bats) are gone.

Mind and body becomes one conglomeration of effort. Nothing is held back during an NFL game because there is no reason to do so. It seems that life can surely go no further than the game clock.

DURING

Halftime is a cruel joke. It is like the taunt of snatching a half-eaten cheeseburger away from a starving man. Even though he will get it back in a few minutes, the emotional plummet is certain. In those twelve short minutes at halftime, the body has just enough time to cool down without getting any rest. The body's systems all screech to a halt. You stop sweating. Muscles tighten. Bruises begin to swell. Torn fingernails sting. Pain seizes joints and tendons. Headaches surge.

Now, more than anything else, is when technical adjustments are made. On occasion, a coach may spew forth an irate speech, but they are rare. I remember one threatening outburst.

"You sons of bitches better get your heads out of your asses! If I see an effort like what I saw in that first half again, I'll personally hit somebody in the head with the damn bench. And you bastards better believe that I'll cut some of your asses on Monday. I mean it! Now get your asses moving…."

One of my favorites was a Jerry Glanville speech when we were getting hammered by the 49'ers. "This game is over", he told us. "I know and you know we aren't going to win, and I don't care. I will tell you this though: I'm not going to look at the first half of this game on film and you won't see it either. As far as I'm concerned, this thing never happened. But I'll tell you this, I'm gonna look at this second half and see who's with me. I'm gonna look to see who's still playing, even though this thing is out of reach. If you lay down on me, you're finished. If you go out there and fight your asses off, we'll be okay. We may lose this, but if you fight there'll be another day."

We did and there was. The next season, we went on to sweep the 49ers, beating them twice, earning a playoff birth and eliminating them from the postseason for about the only time in the decade.

During a winning effort, a coach may sound like an indigent gold miner who just struck a vein of a mother lode.

"We got 'um! We got 'um right where we want 'um! Now don't let go! Let's get back out there and finish these bastards off!" (The only thing missing was a bellowing Yahooooo!)

More than any motivational speeches, it is strategy that must be addressed during halftime, plays that must be stopped, coverage that must be changed, blocks that must be made. Players are urged to drink. If necessary, quart bags of IV fluid are slugged into veins with needles that seem the size of ballpoint pens. Occasionally, some madman will slam down some stadium food – nachos, dogs, or sodas – but only if his stomach is made of cast iron. Most players are leaning back against some wall or locker, panting, dazed, with their heads lolled to one side or the other, like a bunch of convicts catching their breath after a jailbreak.

As soon as the last switch in the body is thrown down and exhaustion has fully registered in the brain, the two-minute warning comes. Everyone rises slowly, shaking and stretching the blood back into their joints and limbs. Even though a player now feels like an old jalopy with a worn-out battery, winding up its motor on a cold November morning, in just two minutes he must be running at full speed once more. When the ball is kicked high and long a second half begins, the gears are all whining in a panicked chorus of energy. The rage and determination are right where they were when you left the field only a few minutes ago. If a guy jammed his fist under your facemask on the last play of the first half, you will be sure to forearm his ear hole on the first play of the second. Everyone picks up where he left off. There is none of the anxiety of pre-game. This was nothing more than an ill-conceived pit stop.

AFTER

When the victor leaves the locker room, he has a spring in his gait. Even if only for a day, he has elevated himself in the eyes of the world. He is a winner. For the loser, his feet feel weighted in blocks of concrete. He is somehow lower than the lowest, open for ridicule and criticism from every quarter. But this, too, doesn't last. There is always next week to worry about. Every veteran of the NFL knows the saying, "You're only ever as good as your last game." How true."

* * *

HALFTIME BOOK PROJECT
INTERVIEW WITH TIM GREEN
(Conducted by Don Grossnickle)

From a former college and pro player's perspective, does the coach's leadership affect the motivation at halftime?

Yes, for sure. I can't recall a certain circumstance, but it is always a critical time from an emotional standpoint. It is a time to get guys to rally up emotionally, along with setting a strategy to make adjustments to the things that are being done by the other team.

The coach's job is to strategize and counteract. Halftime is part of the game.

It is required; since it is there, you have to use it to your advantage. If you don't, or if can't, chances are the other team is going to defeat you. It is there. It's not a matter of whether you like it, or don't like it you have it. It is part of the game.

If everything is working according to the way the game plan is drawn up, halftime is just for taking a drink of water and a matter of keeping things going in the same positive direction.

If something unexpected has happened, or if something is happening that is going to cost you the grasp of your success, it is imperative that you adjust. The coach had better get the team to adjust and use? that time to evaluate where you are and evaluate how the team is going to succeed. It is possible that you might have to change everything. The whole game plan might have to be changed. You might have to shift. The teams that have that kind of flexibility – the teams that are good enough and disciplined enough to adapt – those are the teams that can go into halftime behind and come out in the second half and win.

Does the coach and the style of the coach's halftime pep talk before re-entering the field, matter?

Yes, for sure. It is the coach's show. Everything the coach does is significant.

Is the fire — the flamboyant, emotional halftime talk — a thing of the past?

No, I don't think so.

I think those are still a part of the game. Attitude, spirit and motivation are essential.

Is there a metaphor that describes the role played by the head coach at halftime?

Yes. The military general is the traditional metaphor that comes to mind.

As a player, I definitely see myself playing out a battle. It is a physical contest. I think halftime is an effective metaphor for the matter of how a person deals with life challenges.

Oftentimes in life, we set out a plan. We have an idea of how things are going to unfold. And for most of us, there comes a point when we realize things didn't happen the way we thought they would happen. I think it is important for people to be able to stop and take time out from everything they are doing and evaluate where they are.

They must decide where they're going from here – and assess what is working and what isn't working and consider shifting his or her strategy. If everything is going just fine, just keep going and emphasize the things that are working and realize they're enabling you to succeed.

If there are things that are not working, or things we need to make adjustments to, then face up to the task. Be honest with ourselves. Determine where we are, what we can do, what we cannot do. A person should be able to reflect and not be ashamed to shift their main strategy.

It is not a defeat until the game is over.

Any obstacle that gets thrown in your path – any kind of setback – can be analyzed. If you pause and figure out the options, not being ashamed, maybe you can see a way to make something work. Then the game is not over and you can succeed. You can still win.

Is the locker room agenda or "tone" different in the pros than in college?

I think the college game always is a little bit more emotional.

I think that the professional game's focus tends to be more on looking to gaining a strategic boost. There are elements of both factors active in each level.

Is the focus of halftime geared more for the individual player or the whole team?

Both are important. Each part of halftime is important and not separate from one another.

You have the individual as a focus for adjustment, and the possible adjustments to be made in the context of your position group, and then the entire offense or defense and then the team as a whole. All the elements are important.

Any advice to these paralyzed boys or others in their own "halftimes"?

Not to diminish the gravity or the impact of what these players have had to face – but I think they, and myself, as athletes have found that the most significant aspect of living a meaningful life is found in the intellectual and spiritual existence rather than the physical side.

Even though their physical world has been grossly debilitated, there are a lot of rewards out there – and a lot of very satisfying and important experiences for them in the intellectual and spiritual world. I would encourage them to shift their focus, shift their strategy and work and to compete and train those arenas of the mind.

They still can, in their status, reap some of the greatest rewards that await all of us as human being on Earth. Rob and Rocky can take a journey – if not an athletic one – and pursue a new direction. Every athlete must come to grips with limitations in the face of life goals: How I am going to be productive? How am I going to feel good about what I do? Now do I grow?

For me, the bulk of my accomplishments are in the realm of intellectual and spiritual. Athletes have to turn away from the physical world. My bigger focus has nothing to do with my outlook on being bigger, better, faster, stronger and more athletic.

The physical aspects of our lives tend to pale in significance to the other elements. In today's world, in the history of the human race, a person has access to so much out there – including interaction with other human beings – so that he or she can become accomplished in their existence. I have always just wanted to succeed in my heart.

"Failure is not fatal; failing to change
will be...."Sports do not build character. They
reveal it."

John Wooden

3

Halftime, Football and Life

Nick Saban

Head Coach, Miami Dolphins
Former Head Coach, Louisiana State University
2003 College Coach of the Year

COACH SABAN'S REFLECTIONS:

(Based on an interview with Don Grossnickle and Coach Saban's reflections described in: Nick Saban with Sam King, Tiger Turnaround-LSU's Return to Football Glory, (Chicago: Triumph Books, 2002)

Halftime is wide open for engaging in significant moments with the team. Motivating players sometimes involves words and speeches, and sometimes other things a coach does can potentially inspire the team to greatness. I can recall a situation when LSU was playing Tennessee. They were ahead 14-7. We had a fourth-down-and-inches situation on our own 23-yard line. I called the play. I directed them not to punt and sent in a play. We fumbled the snap.

My whole life flashed in front of me. I blamed myself and could foresee I had made a huge mistake. Mysteriously, however, the defense became inspired by the apparent confidence I had shown to the team, and it became an outstanding turning point that I always will remember. Somehow, this fourth-down gamble of mine aroused both the defense and the offense. The team subsequently put together its best assault and played poised – relentlessly, confidently operating with the precision of a finely honed, well-oiled, polished football-playing machine. This blessing in disguise – a move I'd made without uttering a word – led to a 31-20 win over Tennessee that day. After the game, the players told me the decision I had made to not punt the ball provoked them to think they could win because I simply had shown enough confidence in them to go for it. At the same time, word choice does matter in motivation.

* * *

And it sometimes takes imagination to get the proper focus. Great inspirational talks often motivate teams to accomplish what had been thought impossible. A stirring speech by a coach or a mentor can bring out everything that lies in the heart of a man. Sometimes, something totally unexpected inspires men to go beyond their capabilities, broaden their horizons and transcend the sea of defeat and move mountains.

I learned some of my lessons about motivation and halftime from other coaches. My father was a great motivator and coach. He spent a lifetime coaching Pop Warner youth football. My dad would make a 3 or 4-mile run in a bus to pick up kids and give them a chance to play a game he truly loved. In that bus, I received many motivational lessons. I remember to this day the signs posted all around the tops of those windows, saying things like, "It's nice to be important, but more important to be nice," and "Quitters never win and winners never quit."

The signs were everywhere. My dad was such a tough man – a hard-nosed Vince Lombardi-type – not just to me, but also to all the kids. I learned many powerful lessons from him. I learned that a person has to work hard and you have to do it right. His standard of excellence was so much greater than I always thought it should be or needed to be at the time. Yet, I have come to respect his wisdom: that the ideals we pursue should be reached for, though they might, in fact, be beyond our reach.

* * *

I look back at my beginnings as a coach and remember my days at Kent State as a player for Coach Don James. Coach James was a stickler for detail. He was well-organized and had an extremely strong work ethic. He talked to us in the locker room and on the practice field about things that are important to be successful – as a player and person – and they stick with me today. Teams can benefit from looking at wisdom and know who you are and know your opposition.

* * *

Sometimes, I have to break my players out of complacency – and out of what I call the "brook trout stare." The "brook trout" look is like when you catch a fish, and then you look at it. It gives you that blank stare back. As coach at halftime, we sometimes get a lot of blank stares in the locker room. I try and speak to players in terms that actually will sink in. I apply life lessons taken from many contexts. Teams can benefit from knowing, for instance, who you are and what the opposition is. You can underestimate or overestimate. Union General George McClelland overestimated the enemy and didn't cross the river for a year and a half. He prolonged the war. He could have beaten them before he did. He had them out-manned, but he didn't think so. Custer, meanwhile, underestimated the enemy. I always say if you are a fastball pitcher, don't lose the game throwing a changeup.

* * *

At times I am a storyteller. I am always selling our players on the importance of process. I try to sell them on the importance of the second half and, particularly, the fourth quarter. It's all about mental toughness. Once, I told the story about a boxer I knew who fought for the world championship.

He was winning the fight for the first three or four rounds and then he got beat up badly and knocked out. I said, "You were winning, and then you just got pummeled. What happened?" I thought he would say that the guy hit him and hurt him and he couldn't defend himself. Instead, he said, "I hit him with my best shot, and it didn't do anything. It didn't affect him and I just didn't think I could win." *I just didn't think I could win.* That's like "loser's limp": After a bad play, one of my players will say, "I didn't do well because I was hurt." I ask them, how they heck are you going to win with that attitude?

* * *

Places sometimes can be motivating. The chute in LSU's Tiger Stadium is one of them. I've coached in a lot of places, but that chute is incomparable. The boys and I consider running onto that field, to the roar of thousands of screaming fans, a defining moment we'll remember for the rest of our lives. Leaving that chute as Tigers is so motivating. On days of exceptionally big contests, when we're playing teams that are going to be difficult, I find that the players get pumped up on their own. In those cases, my job is to calm them down.

* * *

Sometimes, humor from a coach in a tense situation can help break the ice. I recall one game when I was coaching for Michigan State and playing Notre Dame with all those traditions of "Touchdown Jesus" and all. Our team was kind of small, and we had 12 true freshmen out of the 64 we traveled with to South Bend. We did not have a whole lot of spectacular players. We had come into their stadium somewhat timidly and were greeted by impressively huge players glorified with the band and all my guys appeared totally intimidated. They had that "brook trout stare." We came back into the locker room entering through their chute, with the band playing and Notre Dame slogans all around us. We had to climb about 20 or 30 stairs to get to our locker room and it was tense, to say the least, even before the start of the game. Everyone could feel it. It was unusually quiet. And it was one of the few times in my career that I found myself at a loss for words. There was a knock at the door, and a coach entered, saying, "Well, boys – I don't know what kind of football players they have here, but they've got one heck of a great band."

Everybody laughed, and a sense of relief came from that simple comment to set the tone. It was all about how well we had come to play, and we were about to show them. We went on to win that game, and I learned a good lesson about motivational climate, atmosphere and how a little gesture can have a powerful impact on a huge group of boys ready to play their hearts out for a game they love.

* * *

Your thoughts, your habits and your priorities on a day-to-day basis – not just in one moment of halftime – determine the choices you make and don't make. These choices end up making you what you are. Self-discipline in athletics is being able to do what you are supposed to do, when you are supposed to do it, in the way that it is supposed to be done. To be successful in football, or in life, it takes the same thing. That's why, as a coach, I want every player to have a chance to be successful in life for having been involved in our program. To do that, the players need to take ownership. It has to be their team. When we build a championship-level team, there are three essential components: effort, toughness and responsibility. All three are important, and take little ability at all. When you are a coach, you recognize that most of the principles and values it takes to be successful as a person are the same as those it takes to be successful as an athlete. There's not a lot of difference. We coaches are in the example-setting business. It is important to have integrity in what you're trying to do. That's the only way you can ask others in the organization to believe in the same principles, values and other things instrumental to being successful. In coaching, you have to be a great teacher. I work hard at halftime, pre-game, practice – you name it – to make it possible to move forward and beyond the point where my players began when they came into the program. I have found that tentativeness exists, hidden within players, and they are prone to wondering if football is worth playing. My role is to provide an environment and get them to the point of great accomplishment. I like Vince Lombardi's inspiring statement: "Any man's finest hour, the greatest fulfillment of all that he holds dear, is that moment when he has worked his heart out for a good cause and lies exhausted on the field of battle — victorious."

* * *

Coaching is teaching. Teaching is the ability to inspire learning – being able to get people to get better than they thought they could. Success is based on consistency and performance. You must be willing to stick with it, persevere, to learn from your mistakes, not get frustrated, overcome adversity that life throws your way and have enough pride to try your best even when – especially when – it seems like you won't succeed. Football is for tough people. I always say give 100% effort and play with toughness. Mental toughness means you are not going to be affected by what happens, and you will always be able to make your best plays when the games get decided. We ask players to condition hard. If you're not in good shape, you are going to loaf when you're tired. Vince Lombardi once said, "Fatigue makes cowards of us all. Toughness is going to leave when you are tired and you are going to make mental errors."

* * *

A coach must be able to manage guys, not show frustration, get them to compete, get them to play a full 60 minutes, not look at the scoreboard and not be affected by the last play. You have to be sure your coaching style is positive enough and rewards the players' self-esteem enough so they're not afraid to make a mistake. You can't play a perfect game. You don't want to make any mistakes, but we all make them. The key is your response to your mistakes. That's much more important than the mistakes you actually make.   With victories and last-minute comebacks, I'm always delighted and happy for our team. I am happy after a victory to see our players so happy. But as the coach, I tell them later, "You know what we need? We need our players to focus on what they need to do to get better as a team so that we have a chance to be successful in the future." I communicate that being saved by a lucky break is not my style as a coach.

Miracles are nice, but systematic winning is my preferred style of coaching and life. People say that I drive hard and that I am a real taskmaster. I'm OK with that. Halftime is a time to be systematic and make adjustments. Emotions and goals are essential ingredients at halftime and throughout the game.

* * *

At LSU, we set goals and visibly place them on the wall of the locker room to establish a vision of where we intend to go. We place the goals in a large pyramid made up of blocks. After a game, each player who plays relentlessly with toughness that measures up to his own standard signs the block representing his progress. The blocks of the pyramid are built one on top of the other, representing the opponents still left to play until reaching the top levels – the championships. We see the pyramid every time we get ready to play and every time we are honored to run up the chute to create our destiny. At LSU, we had a motivational speaker come and talk to our team. "You don't always get what you want in life, but you almost always get what you deserve," the speaker said. This statement rings true for me for a lot of things. It seems to capture what it takes to be successful. A successful person in life, and a winner in football, makes commitments and sets the mark for what he plans to do and then demonstrates the ability to persevere and overcome adversity. Overcoming adversity means getting beyond the suffering.

Adversity involves suffering – and sometimes there is no way around it. Often people want to accomplish things, but my philosophy is that you most often get out of life what you put into it. Sometimes we are not willing to understand, or we are willing to accept our failings because of the fact that we have to accept adversity. You don't always get what you want, but you almost certainly get what you deserve.

I have been fortunate to be around people who have to deal with physical difficulties and have been impressed and inspired by them and consider them to be role models. In my life, I have noticed extraordinary persons of courage who face physical problems and overcome them because of their clear zest for life and willingness to do what it takes to attain victory.

When I see this attitude of getting to the point of pursuing what a person wants to earn from life, I am impressed. I notice that these people, instead of waiting for somebody else, or for something else to happen, get into a personal action mode. I notice those who embody this kind of spirit – this kind of charisma, passion and vision – have the leadership ability to affect other people. People in wheelchairs or with other disabilities are courageous and possess the mental toughness it takes to be a winner in life. I would hope that if I had some deficiency or problem that I would have the character that is so strong that the obvious external disability would disappear, and one would no longer see the problem – because of the great character and the positive ability to affect other people.

That character, that strength of personality, is what always shows.

"The pessimist complains about the wind. The optimist expects it to change. The leader adjusts the sails."

John Maxwell

4

Halftime in the NFL Locker Room

Coach Dick Jauron
Head Coach Buffalo Bills, Former Coach, Chicago Bears

Football has been a big part of my life. I grew up around football because my dad was a coach. Halftime is a fascinating part of the game. In this chapter I share my views about various aspects of halftime. Each of the participating coaches may approach halftime from slightly different perspectives.

Common themes emerge as well. I will use a question-and-answer format because it will allow me to express my perspectives as if you the reader were sitting across from me in my office, or standing with me on the sidelines at practice. Here goes...........

(Interview by Don Grossnickle)

What are your recollections from high school or college football days about halftime in the locker room?

My halftime roots are pretty well set in my high school days. In fact, my favorite story and inspirational moment in my career thus far took place in high school football. I played at an awfully good time at my school in Massachusetts. Sports were stressed, but no more so than academics. It was a really nice mixture of priorities supported by teachers and coaches all on the same page and stressing things of importance. My coach was Stan Bondalevich, who had a great staff. Stan was an outstanding motivator of young teenage football players. Coach was very good at what he did. He would get us very fired up for about every game that was important. Coach was pretty honest with us. He was a storyteller and was very colorful and theatrical.

Once, before a game, he really inspired us. He told us we were a "really good football team" and that we had to beat this opponent — *just because we were better*.

I hadn't heard that before and haven't heard since. I have never heard a coach explain that a team has to beat the opponent *because they are just not good enough to beat you.*

That took guts. Everybody is afraid to make that kind of a comment but he was very truthful and forthright.

We did win it and we won the next one. Coach had a couple of great halftime speeches. One of the greatest was about his son. He would build up to this climax where he would be very emotional and tell you that he felt so strongly about his football team and this group of people that if his own son could ever grow up to be a teen age boy like the boys in this room with the special character, the work habits and the willingness to sacrifice that this group had, he claimed he would proudly be one of the happiest fathers in the United States of America. It was always a very moving speech. By your senior year you had heard it three times and it was still an incredibly moving speech.

Another talk was one he never gave to us. We were ahead 24-0, and at halftime he sent a messenger to our locker room to convey his disgust with our performance. He withheld the entire coaching staff and we did not have a coach in our locker room at halftime. We just had this messenger show up who said, "Coach Bondalevich and the other coaches are not coming to the locker room because they are thoroughly disappointed with your first half. You are not playing anything like you are capable of playing as a football team, and you need to pull yourselves together.

That was one of the best halftime "non-talks" we have ever had. As a result, we became mad. We actually got together to try and figure out what we needed to do better in the second half. We went out and ended up scoring something like 56 points in the game and we won it. I reflect and think that the coach demonstrated great strength in what was *not* said, and there is sometimes great wisdom in what is not said and what is conveyed as much as there is in the words that are spoken. I think that in the locker room at halftime, there is great message in how things are said, where the circumstances that surround what is said and the inflection – the way things are delivered – there are powerful messages in all of that, not just the word.

My coach at Yale University was Tom Cozier. He was very straightforward and always very organized. He reflects many positive ideals that I pattern my views after. He was not predictable. He was generally calm and a team player. He was close to his staff. He was smart and understood that the locker room at halftime is a very emotional room – so you want to be direct, simple and imaginative.

Is halftime significant in professional football?

In the National Football League, halftime is really significant – it is only 12 minutes.

From the time you leave the football field until they come and knock on your door and say you have to be out, it is a 12-minute period. In the NFL there are 53 active players (in a team); 46 are active on Sunday. In high school and college those numbers are bigger. So you have this large group coming into a locker room at halftime, and they all have various things to do and take care of. Some may need to go see the trainer, another may need to be re-taped, and another may need to replace a piece of equipment. They may have to replace part of their uniform or use the bathroom. There are lots of things they have to do – all as part of that 12 minutes.

The staff in the meantime groups together into offense, defense and special teams. The head coach is going to each group individually and that all falls in the 12-minute time. Then, you disperse to your groups and you start talking about the first half and then, with about a minute-and-a-half left, the head coach brings them back together. Lots of things have to get done. The whole thing has to be very organized for that 12-minute period. Halftime speeches or talks are generally strategy, additions and deletions, game plan adjustments, explanations. We take a look very quickly at what went wrong, why it went wrong, what went right, why it went right, why we are going to keep doing it or not doing it. Occasionally, you will get a rare halftime where you will throw all of it out – all of that information and stuff out – and you just focus on an issue. When that happens with us, it has usually been because we haven't done very well and you feel, as a leader, that something is missing. Generally, it might be the intensity of effort. When that happens you throw everything out – forget all of the strategy, all the additions and deletions. Because it doesn't pay to do anything like that. If we are not getting the effort, we've got nothing. We have nothing.

The integrity of our game is the effort that is put into it. The effort with which we play is essential; without it we are nothing. Halftime is generally less motivational and more instructional: additions, deletions, game plan strategy. Pregame talks would be more reminders and more motivation. Which of these is most important? I think halftime is the most important because my view, quite frankly, is that if I have to motivate you to do your job then you are probably in the wrong business and I probably picked the wrong people. You better be motivated. As head coach, I can help direct, point out, try to add to the situation. If you are not ready to play when we come in to the stadium on game day, then my belief is that I have the wrong guys, or I haven't done my job all the way through the week.

What is the main role to be played or job of the head coach at halftime?

I am a strategist. It sometimes is like the role of a parent watching their child develop. It might be like a parent sitting a child down and talking about directions, what has happened and from my point of view what I see. I mention the things I see occurring. I step in and say, "We need to direct and focus attentions in another direction." I see the head coach as a teacher in a classroom. My job is to clarify: "This is what we need to concentrate on … because of …" I reinforce that these are our goals, and in order to achieve our goals this is what we have to get done on a daily and weekly basis. Here is where we are; we need to make some adjustments.

The head coach assumes any role. He could be the priest, pastor, friend taking another friend aside – saying, "Listen, this is what I see. This is what I believe. This is where I think we need to go. What do you think?"

At halftime I just say, "Men, this is what I saw. You saw it, I saw it. We have to correct it. This is our goal." Everything we do, we try to make it simple and make it excellent and have imagination. In the halftime mode you define the situation, accurately, concisely, remind them in the way that is most suitable. We reinforce that we are pursuing excellence;

that is our goal with every player, every play, and every position. Then we try to use our imagination to convey the points and try *to stir their imagination to see what they can do! Use their imaginations to see what they can become!* I see this halftime no different from every walk of life. Halftime just happens to be in the midst of an emotional game. It is a game. It is a game that we are really excited about playing. We see that we have either done really well in the first half and we have to continue that emotion – or we see that we have done poorly. In that case, we have to identify the reasons and correct them in the second half and do a lot better.

Do coaches have a typical style of halftime conduct?

I think that coaches vary their styles. You are generally centered in who you are. Sometimes coaches become an actor portraying somebody deep inside that they are not. I happen to believe that people are very perceptive – especially athletes. If the coach tries to fool them, I believe they see through that. The players do not want dishonesty in people. They want honesty. As the coach, you are who you are. There are times when you as the coach become emotional and one day you will get carried away. When you can't help yourself, or don't want to help yourself or you plan to act in a certain way because you perceive that they need it. I believe that as a coach, you should do whatever you believe is suitable to help them succeed. If it means getting out of character, then get out of character. Your clear goal is to make them better, and whatever that takes to do that, that becomes the role of the coach at that point.

As the final seconds of the first half wind down, what goes through the mind of the coach?

The time is so limited that there is no time for a harangue, that's for sure. The assistant coaches mobilize with their groups. With about a minute-and-a-half left, I call the entire team up and address the whole team. At that point, I have my impressions, the coaches' impressions, views from technology, everything that occurred in the first half. Some things in my final comments I will refer to specifically. Some things I will mention generally and then I will address the second half ahead. I direct what I believe we need to get done. This final talk must be done simply and with some imagination because you want to convey the points and *stir their imaginations* with whatever you say. It is essential that they know exactly what we want and that they become confident that we are capable of getting it done.

There is not a lot of time. The picture I have of myself as coach is that I am part of them and that we are in this together. I do not have a favorite speech or cliché or theme. I do move to expressing feelings. I vocalize my feelings linked with what we have to do to correct things.

I do not specifically plan a halftime talk – other than to carefully organize time and tasks of the 8- or 10 minutes leading up to my final comments. I rarely compile a list of things that I definitely have to bring up at halftime. That's never occurred to me until I leave the field and check my notes. I do use my imagination to make a clear statement – possibly with a motivational, thought-provoking and attention-getting tool that comes to me to apply to the moment. My personal favorite theme or motivating thought: "If there is no wind, row!" Halftime is a time of emotions. It involves people who care deeply about the game.

What kind of coaching comments or motivating message might you offer to Rob and Rocky or other persons in a halftime status of some sort who are facing challenges outside of football?

I have spent my whole life in sports. I love it. There are certainly characteristics of team sports and even individual sports that teach participants worthwhile lessons applicable to various aspects of life. The No. 1 factor is discipline. If a person wants to be good at something, he or she has to want to be disciplined enough to work at it. Commitment is another factor. In order to be disciplined, you have to commit time and you have to be organized and prioritize time.

Teamwork in a game like football is essential. Without teamwork and cooperation, you cannot function without every guy taking some sort of responsibility to do his job and hold up his end of the bargain. These principles are the bedrock foundations of what we do. There are other issues that come into play – such as character. Character is the most important issue in your life. Character leads to faith and drives your commitment to family and community and service to other people. These are building blocks in football that can be applied to life. Those who have played sports – who have had people on you driving you to perform, for you to be at your best to push you and to motivate you and encourage you to practice and get it done – certain levels are not acceptable. Demands have to be dealt with. There is a bar that must be set to establish standards. The coach and management set the bar and the organization works together to accomplish the goals that are set into place.

"Permanence, perseverance and persistence in spite of all obstacles, discouragement, and impossibilities: It is this that in all things distinguishes the strong soul from the weak."

Thomas Carlyle

5

Coach Randy Walker and Pat Fitzgerald: Halftime in the College Locker Room

Maintaining Focus: Keep <u>The</u> Main Thing <u>The</u> Main Thing

Coach Randy Walker
Northwestern Wildcats

Coach Randy Walker of Northwestern University has studied motivation as a way to enhance his coaching effectiveness. **"Keep <u>the</u> main thing, <u>the</u> main thing,"** Walker says. in an interview with Don Grossnickle. "This is a favorite mantra that creeps into many of my halftime talks.

As a matter of fact, I give myself this pep talk frequently. Half time is a moment of re-centering and charting a new course for everyone on the team. The halftime message I typically give to my players is being composed all throughout the first half of the game.

Halftime will be a time for re-orientation, a time to strengthen priorities. Football is so much a game of emotions. The job of the coach is to see through all the emotion and passionate stuff and set a course.

Halftime is, in a sense, a time to navigate. Just as a sea captain must navigate stormy waters and high winds that threaten to keep him from his destination, the head coach makes strategic plans and adjustments. I feel it is important for the head coach to be completely concentrated and focused on the game.

Naturally, there is time during the half for hype and spirit, but intellect and keeping a clear eye on attainable goals must prevail. We should all hopefully leave the locker room intent on carrying out a clearly communicated plan. The interdependence factor mandates that every person knows and carries out *their main thing* – which helps the whole team achieve the main thing. This is easier said than done so much of the time.

The problem to be solved in a football contest is that, in the heat of the battle, opponents have their own plan. This very apparent conflict is probably what makes the game so interesting and challenging. The dynamic interplay of skills, talent and spontaneity spell the difference. Unexpected penalties and injuries contribute mightily to the course of the game; all the unpredictable forces set up challenges that must be faced.

The advance plays and sequences are all laid out as a result of practice and chalkboard sessions. In reality, however – in the heat of the moment – the vision of the 'main thing,' the top priority, must be maintained as central and paramount or confusion and bewilderment will set in.

Doubt and lack of confidence are potentially destructive forces that can work against a coach and his players. The messages and commitment of a workable plan during halftime provide a blueprint. The architecture of the solid plan guides the players and the team to build the victory – play by play, one important moment at a time.

During a game, there must be thousands of mental stimuli that bombard the coach's brain. It is incredibly difficult at times to tune out all the extraneous distractions that threaten the success of the well-crafted plan of attack. Moments before addressing the entire team, the head coach and his assistants often confer and reach a point of consensus. The head coach must thoughtfully and carefully design the messages to be delivered. I try also to be mindful of how the message will be delivered.

The silence of the players, often bruised and battered, fighting off cramps and waves of pain, needs to be broken because the coach will speak and hopefully guide them – say something significant to each of them, motivate them, assure them, refocus them, clarify, encourage and ignite their spirits and unleash their character.

Halftime is a big challenge. Keeping the main thing the main thing applies whether we happen to be ahead at the half 24-0 or are suffering a bashing loss 30-7. The second half offers new opportunities and new moments. Believing in oneself, believing in the plan, believing in one's teammates constitutes so much of the essence of the game of football.

The majority of players that enter the college locker room at the half have been there before. They often have memories of games gone by – both good ones and disasters. Keeping the main thing the main thing is a steady and dependable halftime speech I have used many times. It never gets stale. The football players must maintain composure while using energy and spirit to put them on the line.

The game seems straightforward: "Gain yardage, keep the opponents from scoring and ultimately put more points on the board than they did. Keep the opponent from gaining any advantage. It all seems so simple, but it isn't.

Keeping the main thing the main thing is a decision – a conscious decision that more often than not (thank God) has led my teams and me to victory."

Coach Pat Fitzgerald

Pat Fitzgerald is the current head coach of the Northwestern University Wildcats football team. He was appointed after the unexpected death of Randy Walker. Coach Fitzgerald was 31 at the time of his appointment, making him one of the youngest coaches in the Big Ten Conference and in NCAA Division I-A Football. Fitzgerald starred at Linebacker for the Wildcats in the mid-1990s, helping to lead the team to the 1996 Rose Bowl. Fitzgerald was unable to play in the Rose Bowl, however, after breaking his leg in the next-to-last game of the 1995 season, in which he led the Wildcats to a 10-1 regular season record. Fitzgerald returned for the 1996 season, leading the Wildcats to the 1997 Citrus Bowl.

In his playing career, he twice was named Big Ten defensive player of the year and won the Bronko Nagurski Trophy and Chuck Bednarik Award for the nation's top defensive player.

After graduation, Fitzgerald briefly played with the Dallas Cowboys. He joined the coaching staff at the University of Maryland in 1998. He then moved on to Colorado under his former Northwestern coach, Gary Barnett. He coached at the University of Idaho before returning to Northwestern, where he served as linebacker coach and recruiting coordinator until his promotion to head coach. Fitzgerald greatly admired Coach Walker as a mentor.

(Interview by Don Grossnickle)

Coach Fitzgerald: Soon, you will launch into your new role as the leader of halftime for the very first time. What will be your thoughts about performing the halftime coaching role? What will be your "style"?

First and foremost the head coach must determine the status of the team as we enter the locker room. Are we ahead or behind? Do we need emotion? Does the team seem emotionally high in spirit where I might need to calm the tone down? My job is to gather the status from the other coaches and be able to go out and present a picture and show our young men how we must go out and finish the football game. As I address the ball club, what I'll do is draw strength from all the halftime experiences I have been a part of my entire life of football. I have been playing the game since second grade. I plan to use the key buzz words that we use here as a program to successfully push us through to the second half. If we are down, my plan is to raise them up. If we are too high, I'll need to bring everybody back to reality and then move forward from there.

Coach Fitzgerald: in your view, is halftime in the locker room more a matter of emotion, or focusing on strategy?

I am confident that halftime success involves a combination of both. I think that you need to be able to get done what you need to get done relating to strategy making sure that all the corrections are made for the future going into the second half. At the same time and just as important, it is my job to perceive the emotional state of the program. My job is to work on supporting that sense of confidence. Football is all about muscle and brainpower woven together.

Coach, you have played and coached with some outstanding coaches and mentors; Gary Barnett and Randy Walker, How have they influenced your grooming to be a great halftime leader?

Both of these coaches were phenomenally powerful in successfully finding personal and effective ways to support the team and players. They always found a way to be positive, no matter how deep of a valley we had found ourselves in. They created a positive spin, and promoted a positive message no matter what. They found a way to inspire the whole team, to go out with a vision useful in guiding the performance of the second half. The coaches gave us a reason to head back onto the field with strength and confidence necessary to finish the game.

Coach, do you think that there is a great deal of mythology associated with what is called, "high drama" in the locker room? Do coaches really throw temper tantrums? Do coaches really throw clipboards and such?

I feel that usually, all that stuff is not very good. I feel that all those antics can be more damaging than being helpful to the players and program. It is my opinion that if a coach is going to do some "theatrics" of that nature he had better make sure that he is right in choosing that action for the moment. It is much more important for the coach to have everything strategically well adjusted before showing intense emotion like that. To be practical, the coach better think twice about breaking an clipboard, he just might need it to do some coaching in the second half.

Is there a humorous halftime memory that comes to mind?

Yes, for sure. When I was a player we were playing Michigan in 1995 and I recall getting really sick at halftime. I found myself coming out of the washroom area and I was shocked to see that the whole team had left the locker room area. I was left behind. The coaches had finished breaking us down into our defense and offense and I got suddenly sick. I stepped away from the group. After a while, I hurried and composed myself and came running out of the tunnel only to see that the football was already in the air. Thank goodness we were going to kickoff return rather than going on offense.

I don't think that any of the coaches had noticed I was still up in the locker room being ill.

Coach; please describe Randy Walker's style at halftime?

Randy Walker played things pretty much standard. He taught me all about calming things down. Randy taught me how to concentrate on setting forth a vision that will do a great job of getting the team ready to play on to the second half and be ready to win. I take great wisdom from these two mentors, Walker and Barnett. Both coaches set a philosophy where halftime wasn't so much about theatrics, but instead called forth a mastermind strategy for getting the players to the right place, the schemes and the systems in the right alignment. Randy's "keep <u>the</u> main thing, <u>the</u> main thing" was classic. I will always remember that he stressed the focus on priorities. Coach Randy Walker was a master of concentration and had the ability to get the team to maintaining focus on the adopted game plan.

Do you have a mind's eye mental picture of the metaphor of halftime?

Yes I do. I feel that halftime is really a lot like a boxer. In the first few rounds the boxer has figured out the opposing boxer's game plan. The secret to victory is to come out after the rest and jump on it at the first whistle. So many games are turned around at halftime because the success of attending to the attitude of the football players and the halftime magic.

That precious time can make a difference and every player and coach knows that those few minutes are so critical and important.

"There are no great people in this world, only great challenges which ordinary people rise to meet."

William Frederick Halsy, Jr.

6

Mr. Intermission: Coach Al Groh

Motivating through "Collective Mentality"
Coach Al Groh, Virginia Cavaliers

The media described Coach Al Groh of the University of Virginia as "Mr. Intermission" because of his skillful coaching and ability to perform motivational magic on his players in a halftime locker room. Here's what Groh has to say about halftime, leadership and life.

(Interview by Don Grossnickle)

Why do you believe the media gave you the "Mr. Intermission" title?

Over the last three years or so, our teams have had a number of games where we have come from behind in the second half to win. We had that well-documented Monday night game against Miami when I was with the Jets. We also had come from behind that same year to beat Green Bay, New England and a couple of other teams.

We have had the same occurrences of comebacks here at Virginia. We had a stretch here last year where we won four or five in a row when we came from behind in the second half. One game, we were behind 21-0 at the half. In another, we were down 27-10 at the half. So with this pattern in mind – that is why our team has become associated with intermission strength.

As head coach, you are on record as being humble in accepting little praise for your ability to turn things around after the half. Why is that?

We talk a lot in this organization about having a 'collective mentality.' This feature of ours pertains to many situations, whether it is the approach to pre-season and training camp or the collective mentality it takes to win a particular game or the recognition of a situation in the course of a game. It is not one, it is not 10, it is not 25 – it takes the whole organization to have a collective mentality.

Have your abilities and skillfulness at halftime grown and developed over time?

I would think so; it is really more than a halftime skill. I think all this business about halftime adjustments that announcers like to talk about is overplayed. It must be well understood that if a team waits until the half to take care of things, by then a lot of times it is way too late.

Certainly the halftime is the opportunity for the team to *redefine the game*. That is what halftime is. For some people, it is time to get a hot dog and a beer. For other people, it is time to turn the channel to another game. For a team, it is the opportunity to redefine the game as the present circumstances dictate, and so that is what we go and pursue.

Things are shaped along the way. In many cases, those adjustments or that redefinition of the game and assessing how the original game plan is going occurs at halftime however, the second half decisions and the essence of the halftime talk is being shaped well in advance of the actual start of the halftime clock.

Does your halftime style of coaching reflect the style of your mentors?

I never really think of halftime as a matter of coaching style. On some occasions, people have asked me about my coaching 'style' and how it is defined. I always respond the same way – which is, 'I don't know – I just do it.' I leave the definition to other people who might be there to observe it. I just go about coaching the team the way I think it needs to be coached at that particular time.

Do you think that halftime in football is an effective metaphor in exploring the concept of personal leadership in facing life's challenges?

Yes, I think that you are on track with that question.

There are some very good analogies that can be drawn between the game and life. It is not always halftime – everybody's day goes through it, a year goes through it, your career goes through it, your personal life goes through it; many stages must be entered into in order to progress in a positive direction.

An organization or an individual needs to assess where they are, reevaluate the competition and determine what needs to be done at the present time. A coach responds to the moment."

Do you believe that halftime makes a difference?

It certainly has made a big difference in terms of what we have been able to accomplish at this particular point. Without some of the second-half performance we've had that's changed the direction of the game, obviously we wouldn't have progressed to where we are.

Each one of the wins had a situation that was a little bit different. As such, the assessment of the situation results in a different conclusion and therefore the redefinition is a little different every time. During some halftimes, there is not much to be done. In those circumstances, the coach and team is redefining what positives were going on before. Every game counts and has the same significance."

Is halftime more a matter of intellect, attitude, emotion, motivation or spirit?

I think that elements are brought forth in a different proportion each week. Sometimes there is a whole lot of one and not much of the other. Sometimes, it is a blend. Sometimes the proportions change. What is always required is a quick assessment as the half winds down and the teams go into the locker room.

As a head coach, you have to be very succinct in what you try to direct the team to do. There is only so much that the team is able to focus on. The staff has to quickly digest what went on in the first half and come to some very quick conclusions.

The limited time is very challenging. The NFL is only 12 minutes; college halftime is 20 minutes. There is no time to be wasted.

Do you have a favorite analogy of comparing a head coach to another profession?

No. For me, I am just the head coach of the team. It is unique. Yelling at everybody might make me feel good, but I don't know if that always helps the team. When we come in at halftime, we know exactly what to do. I think teaching is what I do best," he said. I've always taken a lot of pride in my ability to communicate with players and to tell them in an honest and straightforward manner what they need to do to get better.

Note: A glittering example of Groh's ability to motivate and inspire his players occurred during the 1994 season at New England, where the Patriots had gotten off to a 3-6 start. Groh decided he would grab an old shovel from his garage and bring it to work the next day. He is known to have told the players "See this shovel, men? This is how we're going to get out of this thing. Everyone take a shovel, and you dig one shovelful at a time." The Patriots didn't lose another game that regular season, reaching the playoffs for the first time under Head Coach Parcells. Asst Coach Groh brought his shovel to every game, keeping it on the sidelines as a reminder of what it took to overcome adversity.

Coach Groh indicates motivation is a key force in winning: Motivation and team cohesion. Motivation and team cohesion are certainly more important in football than in any other sport. How do you plan for this? How can you develop in your players the same feeling of the importance of winning, on the field and in life?

It goes without saying that your players must be motivated. They must want to become the strongest and quickest possible. They must want to learn so that they can perform in the game. Motivation is essential to perform at a higher level in any sport. And no team game requires the type of collective motivation that football does.

It is certainly a game of the heart. As individuals and as a team, we have got to want it! This, too, is an essential of winning. But even with execution and emotion, with the inspiration of the team and perspiration of the hard practices, the team may not be sufficiently prepared to win. Certainly fundamentals and emotion are the foundations for winning – but on the field, more is always necessary. Successful coaches must plan for the unexpected – practice for the possibilities which can turn the game in their favor. Football is a game of inches. Coaching is a race against time.

Is there a favorite quote or theme you use to motivate players?

Not really. There are a few philosophies or concepts that we believe are bedrock foundation things, but there is not a common one. The concepts are there everyday. The most important halftime concept is that you have to have a collective mentality. Teams have to have it – whether it is the first quarter or the fourth quarter. Teams have to learn how to win when it is not easy.

Do you have a weekly theme you use to focus the team?

Every team or organization is going to operate with an agenda. Somebody is going to set the agenda for the team. In some cases, it is the press, the fans, the alumni, the coach, whoever it might be. Very definitely, we want to set the agenda for the team – internally, that is, it is not set by somebody outside the organization.

From the agenda, we try to give the players some kind of direction toward their efforts, saying, 'Hey – this is what we need to do to win the game.' That is part of every team's preparation. Halftime is an opportunity for the team to gain an edge – whether that is just to solidify what you already have been doing or make some significant changes.

If you can do a better job with your halftime, then maybe you have the opportunity to gain the edge on the other team. Halftime is an important part of the game – just like special teams is important, goal line offense is important, third down defense is important. What we do for that intermission break offers the opportunity to impact the outcome.

Do you have any halftime wisdom for Rob and Rocky to use in their halftime preparations for the second half of their life?

I certainly wouldn't try in any way to equate their circumstances to what a team faces at halftime, because their situation is certainly more traumatic and dramatic.

I feel, though, that they do have to find some inspiration from someplace. Even though their circumstances may be a lot more significant than what a football team does, they have to decide that being successful is not easy. Our football team last year did likewise – hopefully Rob and Rocky can find some strength from that.

"Before you can win, you have to believe you are worthy."

Mike Ditka

7

The Motivation Factor in Halftime Coach- Mike Ditka

"Men are measured by their work, by their methods, and their discipline."

Mike Ditka

Based on Interview and research by: Rocky Clark, Rob Komosa and Don Grossnickle

Mike Ditka has declared that he is proud to be a friend and advocate for Rocky Clark and Rob Komosa. "I'll do anything for these boys" Ditka says, and he means it!

Mike Ditka is a legend for his unbridled enthusiasm and unique ways of unleashing his motivational spirit. Let your imagination tantalize you with the thought of being a fly on the wall in the locker room of this passionate-no-nonsense, no-holds-barred coach

Coach Ditka says, "Much has been written and said about me being a great motivator. I don't really believe I am. I think motivation is the most overused, overrated, overplayed word in our society. I don't believe there is such a thing as motivation – at least not in the sense that most people use the word to describe pep talks and backslapping and all that stuff."

"Motivation comes from within each individual. It is a personal thing. It is pride, guts, desire, whatever you want to call it; some people have it in their bellies and some don't. If you want to win, you find people who have that quality and put them on your team. In business, you find good people who relish the idea of being part of something successful, of helping to build it and see it grow. You recruit them and then run with them. An admirer came up to Mozart one time and told him, 'You know, I'd give my life to play as well as you.' And Mozart looked at him and said: 'I did.' See, Mozart wanted to be the very best, so he put his heart and soul into it. He didn't set out saying, 'I'd like to be mediocre.' If you're going to set goals for yourself, then set some good ones. Say you want to be the best and then don't settle for some half-assed effort. Each person must find a way to motivate oneself. See, I've never understood the notion that you don't work as hard as you possibly can, every day. How are you ever going to get better with that kind of attitude? Now, I know I put way too much pressure on myself when I was playing football. It's only a game and all that. But you know, you get out of something exactly what you put into it. And boy, losing better bother you. I don't mean you shouldn't be able to accept defeat, but you shouldn't get to where you are comfortable with it… If you lose, you ought to be gracious about it on the outside. On the inside, though, you better be boiling. If you're not, you're going out there the next time and you are going to get your head handed to you all over again. It's easy to get used to losing, see. And once you accept it, then you invent ways to lose … You know, in a football game you can trick people for a while, but you'd better bloody their noses once in a while. … To me, when you step on a football field, everybody is equal. When you come off it, though, everybody's not equal anymore. Because somebody has won and somebody has lost. Somebody has dominated and somebody has been dominated. I was told to try and make somebody's all-opponent team. First, you whipped those across from you. Then you got around to whipping the rest of them. If things came easy, then everybody would be great at what they did, let's face it. We would have no inferior people. Some people are willing to pay the price. … Well, I really believe it's important for people to understand that there are alternatives. People want a cop-out. Listen, I'm a realist and I talk about motivation, talk about all the things it takes to be greater or are important to win – and people want to use excuses all the time. We have a lot of people that say, 'I can't do it, it's too tough.' Then they watch someone else do it. 'That's too hard to do.' I think it's important because it is your life."

* * *

There are many stories about Ditka and his motivational style: Ditka got his teeth knocked out in a car accident. He went through the windshield and broke his jaw. The dentist told him, 'We can wire your teeth shut but you can't play tomorrow. Or we can pull them.' "Ditka says, 'Pull the sonovabitches.' As it turned out, they had to wire his jaw shut anyhow because it was broken, but he played all the same. According to accounts, you could hear him out on the field breathing through his teeth: 'Hiss-haw, hiss-haw, hiss-haw.' He sounded like a rabid hound. And you could hear that mad dog Ditka cussin' even with his mouth wired shut."

* * *

He once said in an interview about the "Bears and Grabowskis- The Mike Ditka Story in When the Clock Runs Out by Bill Lyon: …There are teams that are fair-haired and some that aren't fair-haired. There are teams named Smith and some named Grabowski. We're Grabowskis. It's about work ethic, an attitude."….

* * *

As a coach, Mike Ditka was filled with passion, emotion, attitude, motivation and raw enthusiasm. He loved the image of being a Bear – a fierce bear at that. The following is the text of Iron Mike's motivational and fiery pre-game speech given in the locker room for Super Bowl XX. (The talk must have worked: The Bears won the game in one of the most lopsided games in the history of the contest, leading 23-3 at halftime and going on to win 46-10 against the New England Patriots.)

Okay, we've got two minutes. You did all the talking last night. The only thing that I want to say is you made your feelings clear on what has to happen. Everybody said it....Gary, Walter, Dan, Jim, Mike. You know what it is going to take. It is going to take your best effort on every play. Dedicate ourselves to that and we should have no problems. Go out and play Bear football, smart and aggressive. If something bad happens, don't worry. Why? Because we're in this together as a football team and we are going to play it for each other and we're going to win this game for 49, 50 or whatever number we have in this room. We are going to win it for each other. We are going to play it for each other and we're going to pick each other up. That's what it is all about. This is out of love for each other. This is your game. Any other intentions won't be accepted. But, you are going to win this game for each other. So let's go out there and play your kind of football.

Let's have the Lord's Prayer. Heavenly Father, we are grateful for this opportunity and we thank you for the talents you have given us, the chance to prove that we are the very best. Father, we ask that you give us the courage and the commitment to use the talents to the best of our ability so that we may give the glory back to you. Father, we ask that you may protect all the players in the game so that they may play the game free from injury. We pray as always in the name of Jesus Christ your Son Our Lord. Amen. Let's go!

Super Bowl XX Locker Room Chicago Bears
Photo courtesy of Chicago Bears

"It's not the size of the dog in the fight,
but the size of the fight in the dog."

Archie Griffin

8

The Many Faces of Coaches and Halftime

Football coaching is all about heart, passion, intelligence and finesse. Fire and desire are a big part of the game. Motivating and emoting are part of the landscape. Some say it is "not rocket science." Hmmmm, can we be sure? Motivating dozens of players and expecting everyone to give their ultimate…..seems tremendously challenging? Who can be the best at inspiring so many different personalities? Who can be the best at praising? Who can be expert in finding just the right buttons to push at the right time?

This is the arena, the crucible of the football coach. The coach that thrives and survives must become proficient at putting on just the right game face; turning up the heat, pouring on affirmation can be mighty tricky and require great skillfulness and understanding of human personalities. Coaching is finding a key to unlock the hidden talent. Real coaching is finding a spark to ignite passion. Finding a way to turn a focus away from a "screw up" and create an atmosphere where players will take appropriate risks and tap into self confidence, That's what the winning coach must do, over and over…..week after week.

One of football's most celebrated coaches, Lou Holtz in his book: <u>Winning Every Day</u>, describes his views on leadership and pep talks:

"I don't believe you can change anybody's attitude with even the most inspiring pep talk unless it is supported by results. I remember when I was in high school my coach gave us the greatest pep talk I ever heard: Knute Rockne would have envied him. I don't think I have ever been as fired up for a football game as I was that night. Then some guy hit me in the jugular vein with his helmet, knocking me flat. Suddenly, I couldn't remember a word the coach had said. I just lay there making little whimpering sounds. As my teammates helped me up, I left my positive attitude lying somewhere on that field."

* * *

According to legendary coach Don Shula, in the book, <u>Football in America-Celebrating our National Passion</u>: "Nothing compares to the feeling of a big football game. Usually, you can sense the excitement and the anxiety the minute you arrive at the stadium, even if it's two hours before kickoff. What has always intrigued me about the sport was the combination of mental and the physical. I think the physical nature of football is what truly captures the imagination of the fans. There's the controlled violence on the field. And the great skills the game requires—the running, the throwing, the catching, and the defending—can be awesome. And yet, with 11 people on each side, and with such a great variety of formations and plays, physical skills aren't enough. You also must be intelligent to play the game. Paul Brown always said, "Football is a game of error…whoever makes the fewest errors wins. The interesting thing is, the good players today are the same sort of guys who were good when I played, and in my early days of coaching. They are the players who are willing to expend every ounce of them to prepare for competition. You have to be disciplined: you have to work hard. There are no shortcuts to excellence in football and there will never be."

Lovie Smith – Head Coach – Chicago Bears
Associated Press Coach Of The Year 2005

The following are my points of emphasis to the team during the halftime experience:

1. Play the second half as a '0 to 0' game whether you are ahead or, behind.

2. Make sure you get the point across to the team that the second half will determine the outcome of the game!

3. Make your adjustments based on what the team did the first half, not pre-game tendencies.

4. I think it is important that your leaders or captains talk to the team while the coaches are meeting and making adjustments as a staff.

5. Finally, I typically talk to the team and give them one point of emphasis for each segment: offense / defense / special teams, to establish a target to correct for the second half. Examples would be offense – run the ball better, or more physical; defense – take the ball away more; special teams – one big return

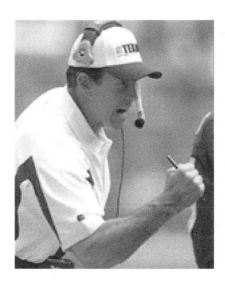

Coach Dom Capers, Assistant Coach, Miami Dolphins, *Former Head Coach of the* Houston Texans *and* Carolina Panthers.

Anyone that has ever been in a locker room during an NFL game knows how fast an experience it can be. Here in Houston, our halftime organization has been outlined and I have assigned an administrative assistant to keep all of the staff and players on time.

It is our belief that when a policy or schedule is on paper it is much easier to adhere to. Our schedule and routine is as follows: we give the players one minute to leave the field and then begin the 12 minute halftime meeting. The first two minutes are set out for the coaches to meet and discuss the first half experience. It is at this time that the coordinators get input from their assistants and then express their own feelings to the head coach. While the huddle session is going on, players use the restroom, get liquids, and see the trainer if necessary. After this, there is a five minute period where both the offensive and defensive coordinator use transparencies to present their overall summary of the first half to the entire team. Here we discuss each series, as well as an overall summary of the first half. Once this concludes, each position coach meets with his players and makes individual comments and corrections. Finally, after 10 minutes, it is my turn, as head coach to address the team.

Collectively I think that people view halftime as a rallying of the troops, a Knute Rockne pep talk, a morale booster, or a rah-rah pep rally, prior to going out into the second act of war. It is not nearly that glamorous. As the Texans head coach, I have preached consistency from day one. Therefore, our team will not be surprised at halftime. No one likes surprises, so our players know exactly what to expect. It is our Texan philosophy that it is easy to do things right some of the time, but it is our challenge to do things right all of the time, regardless of the conditions. This is one of the first reminders we give our team. We do not want them to be up and down like a yo-yo, nor should they expect that from me. That is why at halftime we hold them to the same high standard they were held to at training camp. It is so important for the head coach to have his finger on the pulse of his players, so regardless of the score, my reaction must be indicative of what we need. Newton's Law is that, "every action, has an equal or opposite reaction." We want our players to react to what we say and do positively; therefore, we need to push all the right buttons.

Regardless of the score at halftime we are either going to sustain or persist. We have told our players that it is easy to be great for a series, a quarter, or a half, but we need to be great for an entire game. We need to play each game like a marathon, not a sprint. We do not want to fall into a comfort zone and ultimately lower our standards. We do not want to let our team become casual in anything we do, so therefore we will approach everything we do with a sense of urgency. This could not be more practical than at halftime. It is vital for our players to never be content. Persistence will be the key to our success. Prior to taking the field, we will remind our players one last time of these values, which constitute the foundation of our team.

Obviously, we will change the content of every halftime talk, but we will not change the meaning. We will always challenge our players to be more hungry and driven than they already are. We will never allow our players to relax and take the poison pill of success. And most importantly, we will remind our team of the importance of sticking together as a team. I have shared the following with our team on numerous occasions, and I believe it has significance in any and all facets of life. It is called the Law of the Jungle. (From the Jungle Book)

Now this is the Law of the Jungle — as old and as true as the sky;

And the Wolf that shall keep it may prosper, but the Wolf that shall break it must die.

As the creeper that girdles the tree-trunk the Law runneth forward and back —

For the strength of the Pack is the Wolf, and the strength of the Wolf is the Pack.

We plan to continue to emphasize the importance of both great collective and individual work on the field. The high standard we set on Monday will not be compromised until the final whistle blows on Sunday. The Texans will continue to prosper and achieve success by keeping these ideals and values in mind. In closing, I might suggest that who knows, the next time you turn on a television and notice that we are down by 7 points at half, you too will be assured that we will most assuredly prevail.

Bo Schembechler, Former Coach University of Michigan

The legendary motivator Bo Schembechler set high standards for being known as a passionate coach and motivator. In his biography, <u>Life, Laughs, And Lessons Of A College Football Legend</u>: "Motivation is quite simply the spark that makes somebody do that which he might not otherwise do. You need a ton of it in football. Let's be honest: it is unnatural for people to want to hit each other. You can't just tell a player, "Go out there and cream that guy because I told you to."

Bo says, "Football is a tough, bloody sport, with contact so fierce it can make you wince. If you expect your players to excel, you had better have a good reason, and that reason must be the pursuit of excellence. Not for the individual for the team. You will never get the same level of effort from one man seeking glory as from a group of men pulling for a shared goal. You just won't." I have seen the power of a team. I saw it that halftime locker room in Ann Arbor in 1969, when Michigan was supposed to be chicken feed for Ohio State. Remember Jim Young, pounding on the blackboard…'THEY WILL NOT SCORE AGAIN!!!!!!'

Motivation inspires every comment I made to a player. My job as coach was to know just where and when to say something. Somewhere beneath that crusty exterior the coach must be seen as human. I will not hesitate to cry if I need to". Bo recalls the temper of Ohio State's Woody Hayes. There were accounts of him biting his hand so hard it would bleed. He would yank his hat off and rip it in half. Once before a game I recall seeing him put his fist through a blackboard. Then he wrote EXECUTION. The letters got bigger and bigger because he was getting more and more mad. Finally, he got so mad that, boom! he punched a hole right through it and he had a really hard time getting his hand back out. He sort of dragged the blackboard across the locker room. Then he sent the team out to play.

Kirk Ferentz on Iowa Halftime

"Players, I believe, appreciate a routine whenever possible and we carry that concept to our halftime procedures as well. We typically provide our players time to use the rest room, get re-taped and visit amongst themselves during the initial portion of halftime as the coaches gather and discuss strategy and adjustments collectively. I will typically make a tour through the locker room as the players come in, before I visit with our staff, to share any basic thoughts.

Afterwards, I'll touch base with our coaches to get their thoughts and share mine as well. We try to move as fast as possible thus enabling our coaches to visit with their position players to make any necessary adjustments and also discuss second half plans. About ninety seconds prior to leaving the locker room, I'll speak to the entire team and attempt to provide them with several key points of emphasis for the second half. This might include reminders from our game points as well as important adjustments based on how the game has unfolded.

As a rule, we try to take a consistent approach to our halftime procedure. The exception to this procedure would be if we are not playing with the needed effort or emotion and the players may then receive a little different message and delivery from me, one of our coordinators or position coaches. Basically, halftime is like another meeting with your players, although it can be a very critically important meeting. It gives us as a staff an opportunity to teach, adjust and set the proper attitude to conclude the week's preparation and effort. Often the last half of a ballgame is the most important time of the game week!"

David Cutcliffe
Assistant Coach, University of Tennessee

"Being proactive with halftime is critical to our success. We may not know exactly going into the game what might occur or need adjusting from the first half, but we can make an educated calculation within certain parameters. We will prepare different scenarios on a grease board prior to the game based on pre-game study. This saves us valuable time in talking through what we have seen in the first half. From here, our adjustments are made and we can move on to the players to communicate with them about necessary changes. It goes somewhat like this:

1. Predetermined spot for offensive and defensive staffs prepared prior to game on grease boards.

2. As we first assemble, any chart with information gathered during the first half is added to the boards. Information is discussed and adjustments talked about.

3. Third quarter plan is put in place. We then are off to defensive and offensive squad meetings, individual position meetings, followed by an all-team meeting just prior to departing for the field.

As a head coach, I give my reminders of what we thought going into the game we needed to do to win. I reinforce adjustments made and set an emotional tone to take to the field."

Bobby Bowden, Coach
Florida State University

What follows are the time slot segments and routine we've used for the past 25 years during halftime at Florida State. The time slots are allocated for communication between the head coach, coordinators, assistant coaches and players. Let me explain the substance of each of the six segments:

Segment 1: As head coach, I meet with the offensive and defensive staff separately and then have them brief me on what we must do to win. They will tell me stuff like, "hold blocks longer on pass protection," or "must protect our punter" or "so and so is getting killed" or "we're just getting outfought." From this, I prepare the outline of my halftime talk that comes seven minutes before kickoff.

Segment 2: Offensive and defensive staff continue to confer with each other about what halftime changes must be made or consider if we should consider continuing patterns as is.

Segment 3: Each coach goes to his players, who are seated together, and goes over the adjustments that we must make individually.

Segment 4: Defensive and offensive teams huddle separately and the coordinators of each lecture briefly as to what they must do to win.

Segment 5: This is where I, as head coach, call them all together and give a "pep talk" or challenge to the team as a whole. I may single out individuals or units. This could be a calm 4 minutes or a stormy one, all according to the state of the game.

Segment 6: Let's go get 'em! And we hit the field together. Kickoff will go off in three minutes."

Terry Hoeppner, Coach, Indiana University

Coach Hoeppner relates the story behind the IU locker room facility that holds great meaning and tradition at Indiana University. In 2003, the Hoosier locker room in Memorial Stadium underwent a $250,000 renovation. The facelift to the original 1986 facility included renovating and modernizing the existing space with new carpeting, lighting and a new bulkhead ceiling along with the installation of custom-built oak wood lockers for 105 football players. The renovation was funded in large part by former Hoosier quarterback, Trent Green and his wife Julie.

IU alum Trent Green never forgot the impact Indiana University had on his life. Green, 34, overcame significant obstacles before emerging as one of the NFL's best quarterbacks. He didn't make a pro team his first year out of college and later suffered a devastating knee injury that forced him to miss the 1999 season. "My wife and I feel great allegiance to the school," Green said after IU's entire team gave him a standing ovation at the dedication of the new football locker room facility named in his honor. "To know that the guys here appreciate it means a lot." With his career with the Kansas City Chiefs, he says he's blessed to be in his position. To help replay his good fortune, he created the Trent Green Family Foundation, which helps families with chronically or terminally ill children or seniors.

Paul Pasqualoni,
Former Head Coach, Syracuse University

"There is not much time in football halftime. Separate groups meet – offense and defense. We confirm the perceptions of what the opponent is doing on the field. We then all collectively re-evaluate the game plan in place for the day. The staff deletes and adds to the game plan. Coaching staff meets in depth with their units for a quick few moments. The next focus is to get the game plan for the second half written on the board. The coaches spend time with the players coaching the adjustments. The players quickly meet with their position coach on the specific details connected to their position. The head coach reviews the start of the quarter and lays out what he feels is needed for the team to do."

John Mackovic
Former Coach University of Arizona

At the University of Arizona, the battle cry of "Bear Down" comes from the dying words of a popular student-athlete. John "Button" Salmon was president of the student body, starting quarterback and a talented baseball player as well. The year before his death, Salmon dazzled 30,000 Trojan fans at USC with his powerful punts and fearless play. The recklessness of this hard-rock kid with the curly reddish hair inspired his teammates to nickname him "The Leaping Tuna".

In 1926, on the day before the first football game of the year, John "Button" Salmon, a football and baseball player and student body president suffered a serious spinal cord injury in a car accident. Salmon was driving with three friends when he missed a treacherous curve and spun over a ravine. The others were not seriously injured.

Just before his death on Oct. 18, at St. Mary's Hospital athletics director and football coach J. F. "Pop" McKale visited his starting quarterback in the hospital and asked if he had a message for the team. Salmon said, "Tell them ... tell the team to BEAR DOWN." At Salmon's funeral service, a three mile line of cars snaked from downtown Tucson to the cemetery. A year later the student body voted to make, "Bear Down" the official slogan of all Arizona Wildcat teams. In 1939 the State of Arizona issues a proclamation declaring the phrase "Bear Down" to be the sole and exclusive property of the University of Arizona. The legend of "Bear Down" still inspires Wildcat athletes today and motivates us at halftime by helping us to focus on the pride and tradition that we carry with us each time we take the field. Button Salmon did not get the opportunity to finish out his dream, so it becomes our mission to play courageously in his honor."

Bob Stoops, Head Coach
Oklahoma University Football

My highlights for halftime are aligned with my philosophy:

1. Players relax and get comfortable. Take care of equipment problems. Re-hydrate and eat an energy bar. Coaches meet and make adjustments to present to the awaiting players.

2. Present problems and methods to solve the problem to the players. Also, review the first half and give players the plan for the second half.

3. Finalize adjustments and players get ready to go back out on the field-finish up making personal adjustments.

4. Head Coach will address the team and present the goals for the second half.

Jim Tressel
The Ohio State University

Jim Tressel says, "A favorite motivational quote I'd like to share with the readers of Great Moments in Football Halftime is a statement I have discussed with our team: "We are going to be as good a football team as the class of people we are."

This is a quote from the great coach, Paul Brown. In preparing for the 2003 season I arranged for us to read, "Expanding Your Horizons." The book was written by coaching great, Paul Brown, whom I greatly admire. Players and all staff read it during the pre-season. The book discusses the extraordinary individuals who made up the Ohio State (1942) National Championship team coached by Brown. This form of motivation and inspiration provides a center and establishes a theme that unites our efforts.

As head coach I arranged for the above quote to be prominently displayed in our team meeting room. I set about to make this quote a centerpiece and set the tone for our season. The words are very instructive to players on the field and can apply to the field of life."

Looking back, to 2003, we are proud to say our efforts paid off and The Ohio State University Football team won the Fiesta Bowl, 31-24 double-overtime. The win was a hard fought battle against rival University of Miami. They entered the contest undefeated in 34 games. Fortunately for the Buckeyes, we came out on top. Looking back, the preparation contributed to our teamwork and cohesive focus.

* * *

FANTASY SPEECHES FANS CAN ONLY IMAGINE

Many of us football fans have vivid imaginations regarding just what might go on inside the locker room of the game we are observing. In 2002, a great contest matched the high spirited Fiesta Bowl contenders: Ohio State and Miami. Just after the game an internet hoax published a version of what was thought to be Coach Jim Tressel's pre-game speech. It is included here to illustrate the capacity for fans to use their imagination and take on the imaginary role of coach in the locker room. The speech is entirely fictitious.

COACH TRESSEL'S FICTITIOUS PRE-GAME SPEECH TO THE BUCKEYES.

"Men, tonight you embark upon the last portion of a journey that you started 12 months ago when we walked off the field after the bowl game. Part of the journey involved some of our friends leaving us for various reasons to go their separate ways. But those of you who remain are a part of something special here at Ohio State University. You stayed for a reason. You stayed on because you care about the school, what it stands for, your teammates, and yourselves!

All of you recognize that you are a part of something special here tonight. You recognize that you've come a long way from last January. I encourage you to savor it. Absorb this moment and seize it! Embrace it and take it the direction that YOU want to go. There comes a point in each person's life when he/she asks himself: HOW DO I WANT TO BE REMEMBERED? You have the chance to effect the answer to that question.

The moment is at hand. It is not about tomorrow. It is not about yesterday. It is not about what you did ten minutes ago. But part of your future and how you'll be remembered will be shaped BY YOU over the next three and half hours!!! Look around this room and look at the person next to you. How do you want that guy to remember you? How do you want him to remember the way you played in this game? How do you want your parents, family, and friends to remember your performance on this night? Will you be remembered as ordinary or extraordinary?

Thirty years from now when you have your team reunion you'll see many of these faces again and you'll shake hands. Wouldn't it be nice to be able to grasp the hand of that teammate 30 years from now and you look down at each other's hand and you see a giant ring on the finger? You'll reminisce and you'll soak up the common bond that you have with your teammates that can never be broken.

The coaches have prepared you for this game. The trainers have prepared you for this game. You've prepared yourselves for this game. But there are several things to remember when you take the field:

1. Play with heart. No matter what happens, we don't let up!

2. Play with passion. For many of you this is your last game as a Buckeye. But even for the underclassmen, do not take this situation for granted. Although you earned the right to be here, don't assume you'll be back. Play it as if it were your last hurrah. PLAY EVERY SINGLE DOWN LIKE IT'S THE PLAY

THAT WILL SAVE THE GAME! EACH PLAY MUST BE A WINNING PLAY. As the game goes on each play adds up to a winning performance.

3. *Play within yourselves. Remember what you've been taught and play within that.* So often teams lose games because guys start playing outside what they've been asked to do. Trust your mates and know they have your back.

4. *Have fun! Relish this moment.* Two teams have a shot at this each year. That means an awful lot of young men will go through life wondering what it would have been like to be in your shoes. Enjoy this, men! Don't be afraid to win!

5. *PLAY LIKE CHAMPIONS TONIGHT!* Play with the champion's heart, mind, spirit, & attitude. OWN THE CHAMPIONSHIP, MEN! CLAIM IT! OWN IT! BE IT! DON'T LET ANYONE TAKE THIS MOMENT AWAY FROM YOU! NOT THE PRESS! NOT THE FANS! NOT THE MEDIA! AND CERTAINLY NOT THE MIAMI HURRICANES!!!!! GO OUT THERE TONIGHT AND SHOW THE WORLD WHAT OHIO STATE FOOTBALL IS ALL ABOUT! WE TALK ABOUT THE TRADITION THAT EXISTS HERE! WE TALK ABOUT GREAT MEN SUCH AS HAYES, KERN, GRIFFIN, PACE, & PAUL BROWN. WE TALK ABOUT THE COLORS. WE TALK ABOUT SCRIPT OHIO! YOU'RE NOT ALONE ON THAT FIELD, MEN! THE GHOSTS OF OHIO STATE PAST WILL BE WITH YOU!

All season long we've talked about what it takes to be considered truly extraordinary. What it takes to be considered great! There are people in this world who are afraid to be great! They're afraid to be champions only because they are afraid of the work and commitment required to be in the champion's pantheon! BUT NOT YOU! LOOK AT YOUR COLORS! LOOK AT YOUR HELMETS AND ABSORB WHAT IT IS TO BE A PART OF THE SPECIAL FRATERNITY OF OHIO STATE FOOTBALL PLAYERS! ABSORB THE TRADITION! PLAY FOR THE TRADITION! PLAY FOR YOURSELVES! GO OUT THERE AND BE CHAMPIONS!!!!!!!! BE CHAMPIONS AT OHIO STATE UNIVERSITY!!!!!!!!"

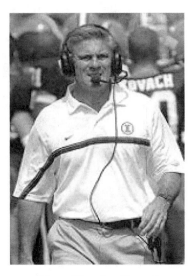

Ron Zook, Coach
University of Illinois

"In the 2005 season during halftime of our first game versus Rutgers, we were down 27 to 20. Nothing was going right, and our players just wouldn't let loose. As I walked into the locker room for halftime, I didn't have a clue about what to say to them. I entered the locker room with my older brother, and I just blurted out "We have them right where we want them!" I could feel my older brother looking at me like "he's flipped out." I kind of caught our team off guard as well. They were not sure what to think. They loosened up, and we were fortunate enough to win the game in overtime."

Zook has quite a reputation as a "motivator." Sportswriter Brian Schafner writes: "Zook is a motivator. Hell, he could fire up a tree sloth if he needed an extra fullback. If the walls of the visitor's locker room inside Commonwealth Stadium could talk, then cue the censor. Coach Ron Zook gave a halftime speech that Woody Hayes, Bill Parcells and

Vince Lombardi would have been proud of. Zook's team was down 14-3 after two quarters and something needed to be done. So Zook let them have it. He screamed at them, challenged them and maybe even cursed at them. Zook's verbal bullets ran into Kevlar Vests as they reached players ears. The motivation did not work this time."

Art Shell, Coach
Oakland Raiders

When going into halftime we will have a presentation from the people upstairs and bring the big picture perspective. They will make a presentation on what the opponent is trying to do to us on first, second, and third downs. Next, we will look at charts that show us patterns detailing where we have been successful in accomplishing our established game plan for the first half. Finally, we will address some pending adjustments we feel we need to make to the experience gained during in the first half.

Lloyd Carr, Coach
The University of Michigan: It's the shoes

In many games, the adjustments (or lack thereof) made at halftime are critical to the ultimate outcome. One of the more memorable halftimes I have experienced occurred in the 1986 Michigan-Ohio State game in Columbus when I was an assistant to Bo Schembechler.

I recall it was a cold gray day in the Horseshoe, typical of the game. The Big Ten championship and the Rose Bowl game were on the line and we went into the locker room at the half trailing 14-6. The players were yelling and screaming because we were having a hard time keeping their feet on the artificial surface. Bo discussed the situation with our equipment manager Jon Falk and then made the decision that every player would change to a different type of shoe for the second half: the 'wet shoe' would provide better footing. Falk was able to get every player into the new shoes, and then Bo personally inspected each player. Bo told the players we were going to win the game and that the change in the shoes would make a big difference in the second half.

We took the second-half kickoff and drove 83 yards with tailback Jamie Morris rushing four yards for a touchdown, the first opponent touchdown in Ohio Stadium all season. After the Buckeyes kicked a field goal to move the lead to 17-13, Morris rattled off a 52 yard dash, followed by an eight-yard touchdown run, to give the Wolverines the lead for good.

Morris rushed for 210 yards and the two touchdowns and helped quarterback Jim Harbaugh (19-for-29 for 261 passing yards) lead the Wolverines to a 26-24 victory. The victory put our sixth-ranked Wolverines in the Rose Bowl with a share of Michigan's 32nd Big Ten football championship. The win also provided Bo his 166th career win at Michigan, making him the winningest coach in Michigan football history. All because of a halftime shoe change.

* * *

SOMETIMES TO MOTIVATE-YOU GOTTA HAVE A GIMMICK

Lloyd Carr-Climbing Mount Everest,-A Season-Long Motivational Theme

Coach Carr creates many great Michigan halftime and motivational experiences. Here is great example of the deep thinking that coaches put into inspiring themselves and their teams. The story is described in Michigan Daily, <u>Carr Rises Above Critics' Questions To Take Michigan Back To The Top</u>,

By Nicholas J. Cotsonika: "Several summers ago, for my birthday, my daughter got me a book about stories from people who climbed Mount Everest," "What it takes to make the climb is similar to what you go through in a football season. Because of that metaphor, we chose that for our team." "The preparation to climb Mount Everest is so important," Carr said of the 29,028-foot ascent."You have to be ready to train hard. Your whole goal is a mountaintop experience. The idea came to Carr after he read Jon Krakauer's bestseller, *Into Thin Air*, the story of a climbing expedition up Mount Everest that ended in tragedy.

Carr wanted his team to concentrate on taking one game at a time, like a climber takes one step at a time, and to rely on each other for support much like climbers depend on each other for survival. The coach invited Lou Kasischke of nearby Bloomfield Hills, a member of Krakauer's expedition, to address the team during preseason workouts. Here are some of the main motivational and inspirational messages: You're committed to a cause that's bigger than yourself. You don't climb by yourself. You climb as a team.

In football, anything you achieve is achieved by the team. It takes tremendous concentration, intensity and focus to achieve that experience. On the mountain, one missed step on one side and you fall off the ridge in Nepal. On the other side, you fall off the ridge in China. One missed step leads to death. In football, even a momentary lack of focus can cost the national championship.

Looking back, the strategy of adopting the mountain climbing story worked well. Coach and players reflect, "We're proof that you can never think something is impossible. That mountain-top experience is something that has changed the life of anyone who went through it. The memories, the lessons and the achievements were so great that they will have an impact on everyone the rest of their lives. "

Biggest Bowl Turnaround – Bob Pruett, Head Coach, Marshall University — — GMAC Bowl Marshall vs. East Carolina

"I am standing on our sidelines, shell shocked at our first half performance. We are down to East Carolina 38-8. Just like Murphy said, "Anything that can go wrong will go wrong." This was by far the worst half of football I have seen out of our club since I arrived at Marshall in 1996.

As the first half is coming to a close, I begin to wonder how I am going to approach my players and staff in the locker room. The game clock now shows zeros, and I start my walk across the field. Immediately, I rounded up my coaching staff for a private meeting in our locker room. I stressed to them the corrections that had to be made, along with how to approach their kids in their position meetings. I told them to remain positive with their players.

As the position meetings concluded, and they were coming together on each end of the locker room for offensive and defensive meetings, I made a trip around the locker room. During my trip, I told players individually that we were still in this ballgame and giving them words of encouragement. The unit meetings have finished and the team is coming together. Finally, it is my turn to address the squad. I stood in the middle of the room, looking each of the players in the eye, and talked to them like men.

I told them to have faith, and that good things happen to good people. I was positive, and told them that even though we are 30 points down, with 30 minutes to go, we were going to win this football game. I even told the players that if you didn't believe me, you can get up and walk out the door right now. No one moved.

I knew deep down that I had reached our guys. The official walks through the door and calls for our captains. As those guys headed out, I had a few minutes with the other players. I stressed staying positive, keeping with the game plan, and doing what you have been taught to do. With the second half kickoff and the clock ticking down, things began to change. We score quickly on a turn-over.

That was the beginning of things to come. Touchdowns and field goals are exchanged throughout the half. After we battled back and trailed 51-45, East Carolina recovers an onsides kick inside of two minutes. With faith, desire, and dedication to not giving in and giving up, our defense has the series of their careers. They stopped the Pirates on a three and out. After the punt sails into the end zone, we now have an opportunity to win the game. Needing a touchdown, and having to drive 80 yards in 50 seconds, without any timeouts, we begin our charge towards history.

Quarterback Byron Leftwich worked his magic and made play after play. Hitting receivers Darius Watts, Josh Davis, Curtis Jones and Denero Marriott we are now within striking distance. With seven seconds remaining on the clock, Leftwich hits Watts in the corner of the end zone. He makes an absolutely unbelievable catch. We had tied the game at 51. Our sideline burst into cheers and excitement.

Adversity wasn't done striking. Our kicker misses the extra point and sends the game into overtime. Swapping touchdowns in the first session of overtime, I continue to remain positive with the players and coaches.

Our defensive holds ECU to just a field goal in the second overtime. Trailing 61-58, our offense heads onto the field. We immediately connect on a 21-yard pass. After two failed opportunities at punching it in on the ground, we go back to the air.

Leftwich hits Davis on a crossing route, a flag flies, we all are holding our breath collectively. Defensive holding was called. The Thundering Herd has rallied to one of the largest comebacks in college football history. This game was also the highest point total in bowl game history. At the conclusion of the game, while speaking to the guys, bowl championship trophy at my side, I thanked them for believing in themselves as well as their coaches, knowing that they would prevail no matter what they were up against, and that if they persevered, they would come out on top – which they did. Every coach has his own ways and methods for focusing the players, yet I have always believed that the effort of the players wins games.

Coaches need to provide strategic approaches that will position the players to make plays, but the players have to get the job done against the other teams' players! You cannot trick your way into victory."

Jim Hofher, Former Head Coach
University of Buffalo

Turning Around A Losing Record

"In the 2003 season, we were receiving plenty of national exposure for having the nation's longest losing streak. As it grew throughout the season, it made for an extremely challenging coaching job of encouraging the kids to simply avoid that distraction, and prepare and focus on playing the game, each game. I absolutely believed that the streak would end, because all of them do at some point! I addressed it only one time during the streak, and it was on the Monday prior to when we finally ended it that following Saturday. (Stupid me, I should have addressed it long before!)

The opponent we defeated is less important than the message that our 5th year senior captain, RT Jeff Mills, delivered as he was leaving our team room for the 2nd half coin toss. He was so determined, and convinced, that we would pull victory from the jaws of defeat that afternoon, that he proclaimed to his teammates that we would sing our fight song when we returned to the team room after that game. Singing the song is reserved only for victory. Jeff is also one of the most reserved personalities on the team, so it was quite a statement of confidence that he was showing to his teammates that we would erase a 17-10 deficit at halftime to win. We did, and it was the most glorious song any of us had sung!"

Gary Barnett, Former Head Coach, Colorado,
Northwestern University

Setting Standards to Achieve Victory

Coach Barnett writes, "Probably the most significant halftime experience that I have had occurred in 2001 when I was at Oklahoma State. We were down 16-7 at halftime. We had just lost to Texas on the road, and if we had any chance of staying alive in the title hunt, we had to beat Oklahoma State. We had lost our quarterback in the first quarter.

When our team came in at halftime, we had nine players hurt in the training room and everyone was yelling at each other. Expletives were abundant. Players to players; players to coaches; coaches to players. I went to the training room to get away from the commotion. I just felt that the team needed to let off some steam and take control of its own destiny at that point.

The training room looked like a "mash unit," and the noise level in the locker room was unbelievable. I remember that after the commotion died down, our offensive line coach,

Steve Marshall, came into the coaches meeting room with eyeglasses bent and he said, "We got 'em right where we want 'em" (meaning our team).

Normally, we are a very calm, businesslike group, but this day was different. They had to vent their emotion and realize it was in their hands – not anyone else's.

We came out the second half and drove the ball down inside the fifteen and missed a field goal. Oklahoma State kicked a field goal, and now we were down 19-7. As had been with our team all year, we took our "We don't care" attitude about what happens to us. We had a goal and a commitment, and we were going to make it happen.

We came back and scored a 33-yard, two-point conversion and won the game 22-19. After our season, everyone pointed to that game and that halftime as the most important event of the season. The other significant halftime event occurred when I was at Northwestern. We trailed Illinois 27-6 at halftime. We just stayed positive in the locker room maintaining composure and confidence and won 28-27. Perhaps the most significant motivation-related event occurred that year. The event occurred just prior to the game. We had just lost to Southern Cal 41-3. We had been booed out of our own stadium. Our quarterback had walked out and we were on the road, in the Rose Bowl against UCLA. After warm-ups, one of our senior captains, Tyler Brayton, was so upset with the lack of emotion in our warm-up that he put a piece of tape across the floor at the entrance from the locker room to the field.

He stood there at 6'6" and 275 pounds and said, "If anyone crosses that line and is not ready to play their heart out, that person will have to answer to me at the end of the game." We kicked UCLA's fanny in 100-degree heat. As a lasting tribute to remember that significant moment we had our Big Twelve North Championship rings engraved with a quote: "We crossed the line."

Urban Meyer, Head Coach, University of Florida-
Formerly Utah, Bowling Green

Toughness and Preparedness

"During the 2001 off season our coaching staff set a tough goal, to make February through March the most difficult eight weeks the players would ever experience, I would remind the players that at some point during our first game (against a Big Twelve opponent), they would be holding hands in the huddle in the second half – battered and fatigued – and look up at the scoreboard and the score would be extremely close. I told them, "For this very moment is why we train with the intensity, discipline and passion that we do."

We had over 20 players quit the program during those 8 weeks. However, for those who stayed, they experienced the biggest turnaround in Division 1A in 2001. We went from a 2-9 program to 8-3. We beat Missouri 20-13 in the season opener. At halftime in that game, the score was 10-7. Our staff reminded the players that *the* moment we had trained for and dreamed of was at hand. I told the team, "The most invested team would win this game." Bowling Green scored two touchdowns in the second half to defeat Missouri and get the season off to a new peak and beginning."

Andy McCollum, Former Coach
Middle Tennessee State University

As the head football coach, I believe that you can talk too much, too often to your football team. For that reason, I allow our players to conduct our Chapel program. I also assign each game to an assistant coach for them to share their inner most thoughts and feelings about the opponent at the pre-game meal. This allows each coach an opportunity to motivate the team and keeps my message fresh.

As a fledgling Division I program we were searching for an identity and respect. We had entered into the arena of Division I competition with a bang, going 3 – 8 our first year. Our second year we improved with our first victory over a Division I opponent and finished the year on an up beat note in the final game by outlasting a future Sun Belt Conference foe in three overtimes to earn our first winning record at 6 – 5.

Our third year we were officially a member of the newly formed Sun Belt Conference and were returning a veteran club with aspirations of greatness displayed in their commitment to prepare and outwork our competition. We were to open the season at Vanderbilt University in Nashville on a Thursday night. Our players were excited at the opportunity to open so close to home against an SEC opponent. All summer our guys lifted, ran, and played pick up games with a renewed sense of excitement and anticipation. As we got further into camp I felt we had a great chance to represent Middle Tennessee State University and Murfreesboro well in our opener, as the sense of urgency and focus on the part of our coaches and players was electric.

My secondary coach was selected to give the opening message at the pre-game meal for the Vanderbilt game. He related the story of the baby elephant. It seems that in the heyday of the traveling circus, the giant elephants were the larger than life attraction that created a lot of excitement and interest in the circus. As the baby elephants were indoctrinated into circus life, they needed to be trained to be docile animals that could obey simple commands. This may not seem like much, but a 3,000-pound elephant can do a lot of damage if he does the unexpected. It seems that in order to get the elephants to begin to understand their role, the trainers will tie them to a stake and only allow them to walk in a circle at the length of that rope. As the elephant grows, the rope is exchanged for a chain, so the bigger, stronger elephant is still unable to break free of his chain. As the elephant begins to reach maturity, the chain is not strong enough to contain the elephant. However, by training, the elephant is conditioned to understand that he was never strong enough in the past to break the chain, so in his mind he knows he is not strong enough to break the chain now. The secondary coach related that the Blue Raiders were the baby elephant in this story. He told the team that we were on the verge of reaching maturity now. MTSU had made good showings in the past couple of years against Mississippi State, Illinois, and especially Maryland. But now it was time to break the chain and do the unexpected. Today was the day to become that 3,000-pound elephant and go on a rampage. Today was the day that we would earn respect, become a team to be reckoned with, and would cease to be "Little Middle". In conclusion, he held up a 5-foot length of logging chain and told the team "Men, it's time to break the chain."

As we had our pre-game meal the atmosphere was charged. I felt we were prepared and ready, but as a coach you never really know until after the game. We came out emotional and sharp, but had the normal first game yips. We were playing even in the first half and pulled ahead until we gave up two long touchdown passes on the same play to the same player on blown assignments. At halftime, as the coaches met to discuss adjustments, one of our senior defensive linemen began a tirade, the theme of which was come on and play harder. Our senior quarterback told him to quiet down and rest up for the second half. Our quarterback then told the team that we've got them down. He said, "They are tired, we aren't. Just do your job, keep your poise and let's break the chain and get our first big win." Everyone just kind of nodded in a quiet, confident way and then the coaches came out and began to meet with the players.

As the second half wore on it was apparent the quarterback knew what he was talking about. We slowly began to take control of the football game. Our tailback began to ramble, gobbling up huge chunks of yardage. Their frustration began to show as they got a couple of personal fouls. In the third quarter, a 16- play, eighty-yard drive seemed to pound a stake in their will. Finally, after an 8-play, 42-yard drive with 3 minutes and 42 seconds left in the game, our quarterback rolled into the end zone at the end of an option to seal the victory.

It was MTSU's first victory over Vanderbilt in 13 tries. We had piled up 608 yards of offense and had rushed for over 300 yards. It was a harbinger of things to come as we went on to finish the year with the 5th ranked offense in the nation. Our final record was 8 – 3 and we were co-champions of the Sun Belt Conference in its inaugural year. Truly, we had broken the chain and started on a rampage, just like the 3,000-pound elephant.

Fisher Deberry, Head Coach, Air Force Academy

Never Give Up

"I can recall two outstanding locker room experiences that remind me of how important it is to never give up – especially at halftime. Both of these experiences happened in games against the University of Utah, in their stadium.

One year, we were behind 35-14 at halftime. It wasn't that our team was playing all that bad, but Utah was playing an outstanding game. My message to the team at halftime was: If you believe you're out of it and you can't win this for sure, we won't … and we can pack up and go home right now. Or, if you truly believe, and I sincerely think we can come back and win this game, we will conquer.

From 35-14 down at half, we played exceptional football and won the game 45-35. And last year in 2002, we were behind 26-6 at halftime. I made the same remarks to our team in the locker room and obviously they chose to believe them in the same way that we had done previously. We came back and won the game 30-26.

I am confident, as it states in the Mater Playbook in Mark 9:23, "If you truly believe, anything is possible." God provides opportunities. It is our choice to never give up and to honor Him in the way we approach the adversities in life."

Paul Johnson, Head Coach, US Naval Academy

Humor Breaks the Ice

"In the game of football, a lot of humorous and funny things happen when nobody is watching and the team is in the privacy of their own locker room.

I recall once we were playing a game where we were coming into the locker room for the halftime break winning 21-4. The opposing team was moving the ball fairly well on offense and gaining momentum. As the head coach started to address the team, he began by saying that the other team is marching up and down the field, first down after first down, and stated that the objective was to play harder and get them off the field.

All of a sudden, the coach was interrupted as one of the defensive tackles raised his hand, and the head coach asked him what he wanted. The player looked at the coach, and in all sincerity, inquired, "How many points do you get for a first down?"

The locker room went deathly quiet, and the entire coaching staff burst through the door, laughing so hard they were crying. We went on to win the game 48-6.

But I've never forgotten that moment and how the player was able to put things into perspective – without even knowing it."

Dan Reeves Former Head Coach Falcons, Giants, Broncos

Superbowl False Start Blues

"Let's reflect back to Superbowl XXIV. It is Denver vs. San Francisco. We were down at the half. My take on the situation was to declare that our mission is simply, "Let's go out and play as if it is 0-0."

That is the message I delivered as we prepared to leave the locker room and take the field. The officials knocked on the door and gave us three 2-minute warnings. We endured three delays and three speeches by me as we prepared to re-enter the field after halftime. I would bring the team up, and give them the talk, and then nothing. The field wasn't ready. It was very frustrating. Not a lot of fun especially when you are down by 24 points. It is painfully too obvious that TV controls a good amount of control over the halftime. The final score was 55-10." This game was painful and it remains the most lopsided game in Super Bowl history to date. The 49ers' 55 points were the most ever scored by one team, and their 45-point margin of victory was the largest ever."

Mark Richt, Head Coach, Georgia Bulldogs

Sometimes Players Are Leaders at Halftime

It is halftime of the Auburn-Georgia game of the 2002 season. We were getting beat pretty bad. While the score was only 14-3, it should have been about 24-0, but Sean Jones had a really good half with a couple of interceptions and a fumble recovery to keep us in the game.

Of course, the game was for the SEC Eastern Championship and at Auburn – a hostile environment – and we were looking like we were going to get beat. As I was making adjustments with the coaching staff, I was thinking about what I might be saying to the team, and I was getting ready to give a kick-in-the-rear-type speech, because I felt that was what the team needed.

But as I was thinking of what I might say as we went over our adjustments, I could hear John Stinchcomb, our senior offensive tackle who was also an All-American, step up and begin to lay into the offensive side of the ball – especially the offensive linemen – and begin to challenge them to play better.

He hit on the fact that we were not getting the job done. John proclaimed to the attentive eyes and ears of everyone that the team was immersed in the kin of do-or-die situation for our team this year and that he had been at Georgia his entire career and never won a championship. He knew that if we didn't win that game that he would never be able to put a ring on his finger. So he basically asked the men to look at the player next to him in the eye and realize that he was letting him down. And if that senior offensive line didn't pick up the pace, then they were going to lose their opportunity to be a champion.

He got everybody's attention on the team. Defensive players heard it in the next room. He made my speech a whole lot easier, and it was a great example of a guy being a leader even though it wasn't a popular decision at the moment. I'm sure his teammates didn't appreciate him calling them out like that, but they responded well and we came back and won an exciting fourth quarter comeback victory to put us in the SEC Championship game against Arkansas – which we ended up winning.

Without his leadership and his actions at half time, I do not believe we would be SEC Champions today!

Coach Dave Wannstedt, Head Coach
University of Pittsburgh

Former Coach Miami Dolphins, Chicago Bears

Coach Wannstedt says, "This is a great kind of funny halftime coaching story I'd like to share. It was in 1987. I was coaching at the University of Miami. We were playing Michigan at Ann Arbor. I believe there were 106,000 people in the "Big House", the largest crowd in ten years. I was the defensive coordinator. There was one minute left to go in the first half. I had been making defensive play calls from the press box. Michigan called a time out so I told all the other coaches to go ahead and make for the locker room mentioning that I would be down shortly.

When the half ended I grabbed by half time notes I had been preparing and headed out of the press box. We were so high up I could hardly see the players on the field. As I began jogging down the ramps somehow I got tangled and lost in the huge crowd. Now realizing myself to be in a full panic and sweating profusely, I finally arrived at the locker room entrance. The door opened and the team was streaking out. Coach Jimmy Johnson just looked at me and remarked how he expected that the team had better play better defensive in the second half. We went on to win the game in the last two minutes of that game." Sometimes, somehow, things work out for the best."

Tommy West, Head Coach, University Of Memphis

My son, Turner, was 13 at the time and had been in locker rooms all his life. As I was the head coach at Clemson, he was used to coming and going as he pleased.

When I became the defensive coordinator for Rip Scherer at Memphis, he didn't understand. We came in at halftime with a 7-0 lead over Louisiana Monroe. We had played poorly on offense and our head coach was furious. After our coaches meeting, I went to our defensive players to calm them down and talk about the second half.

Coach Scherer had walked in and was still upset. He had his back turned and I could see he was preparing to turn around and blast our team. As Coach turns to address the team, I saw my son Turner walking through the middle of the locker room eating a piece of pizza. He saw me and, just as Coach turned to our team, Turner shouted, "Hey Dad – you want a piece of pizza?"

With that, the entire team went silent and I responded, "Not right now." Coach got to begin his halftime adjustments and we went on to win 28-0. The tension was broken and we all took a deep breath and gained perspective.

Mike Martz, Asst Coach, Detroit Lions

In 1982, I was coaching at the University of Minnesota and we were playing Michigan. We were losing badly at halftime. As I was ready to get on the elevator to go down to the locker room, I helped an older woman (in her 80's) in a wheelchair into the elevator. She asked me if I was a coach of the "Gophers", and I replied, "Yes." Her reply back to me astounded me: "You should be ashamed of yourself.... you stink!"

* * *

In the fourth quarter of the first game of the 1995 season, Isaac Bruce had a chance to be the all-time NFL single-season reception-yards-gained leader. He needed just a few additional catches. The Rams were losing by 3 touchdowns with 5 minutes left. Isaac refused to go in the game to get the record. He said the record had no meaning to him in a losing situation. His emphasis was not a focus on himself, but on winning and achieving excellence. He taught us all a lesson."

Ken Hatfield, Former Coach Rice University

It was 1981 in Tokyo, Japan, at the Mirage Bowl between 3-7 Air Force and 5-5 San Diego State. At halftime, Air Force (I was the coach) was trailing 16-0. San Diego State had set an NCAA record of having 68 offensive snaps in the first half. We were getting slaughtered. My big halftime speech was "go to sleep." Both teams occupied the same locker room (separated by a chalkboard), the halftime program lasted over one hour. The second half began and they were stiff from the long halftime wait. Air Force scored on all three possessions and we won the game 21-16.

* * *

In 1992 at Clemson, I was coach and we were playing at Virginia. We trailed 28-0 at the end of the second quarter. Back-up quarterback Louis Solomon broke loose on a 20-yard run to cut the score to 28-7 at the half. I told our team that if they could score 28 points in one half, we could score more in our half. The players bought into it and believed. We missed a field goal, missed an extra point, and got stopped on a fourth down play – but the players were greatly motivated and Clemson won the contest 29-28.

* * *

In 1999, Rice was playing a contest against Hawaii in Honolulu. It was our first trip to the island against a great run-and-shoot team. We trailed at halftime 21-7. There was a quiet confidence in our locker room. On the first play from scrimmage in the second half, quarterback Chad Richardson went 61 yards for a touchdown. Rice went on to do well in the second half, and won 38-19.

Bill Belichick, New England Patriots

No book about coaching football would be complete today without saying well deserved things about Bill Belichick. He is known to be elusive and reserved and not one to willingly enter the spotlight. His outstanding Superbowl victories and coaching genius seem to hinge on to his extraordinary ability to be a master strategist. He has a reputation for being very much in control of his emotions.

In a published interview Coach Bill Belichick was asked by Peter Richmond, GQ, January 2005, if he'd made any adjustments at halftime, Belichick said, " in his usual monotone, "We don't wait till halftime. By the second series in the game, certainly by the end of the first quarter, unless it's a very unusual game, the game is declared." There it is. In a sport whose myths are forged on the feats of astonishing athletes or on inspirational Gipperesque speeches, the best team in professional sports has been built by a man who is, essentially, a systems analyst. More than anything else, Belichick is guided by the modern corporate philosophy—that in an industry where quality is pretty much equal across the board, the most efficient and flexible system will win out. "

* * *

In 2004 speaking at his Alma Mater Belichick reminisced a bit about how things have changed for him as a coach......"I came into the N.F.L. in 1975 from little old Wesleyan," "Nowadays, you talk about halftime adjustments and what goes on at halftime. I'll tell you what went on at halftime in 1975—the players came in and ran right to their lockers and pulled out cigarettes. It was like a Bruce Springsteen concert. But, you know, football has just exploded, and it is so competitive now across the board."

* * *

Belichick is not particularly known for fiery halftime speeches. His skillfulness relates to his ability to analyze his opponents and be resilient and adaptive throughout game play situations.. Without much information available about his halftime coaching style it is interesting to examine his views on the topic of dealing with adversity. In a Belichick Press Conference held on September 21, 2005: Q: Is how a player handles adversity something you don't know, maybe a young player, until you see it in the regular season?

A: I don't know. I think that's a hard question to answer. Everybody has adversity. Football is a game where everybody gets knocked down sooner or later, usually sooner, and then you get up and then you get knocked down again. That's what football is. It's a lot like life in some respects. You're always going to have to deal with some form of adversity in this game. Every team is. Every player is. Every play is not an 80-yard touchdown. Every play is not a strip sack. Some bad things happen on plays. Some good things happen on plays. That's the ebb and flow of the game and it goes like that within a season. It goes like that within a career, just about anybody's career. Maybe how one person handles it at one point and how they handle it at a different point, maybe that is the same. Maybe it isn't. But, everybody goes through it and everybody is going to have to deal with it. Every team has it. Every player has it. Every coach has it. That's just part of it. Just like it is part of life, it's not all roses."

CLASSIC COACH JOHN MADDEN ON HALF TIME

John Madden is one of those colorful coaches people love to listen to. In his book, *"One Knee Equals Two Feet,"* Madden lays out his beliefs about attitude, halftime and the game of football. Coach Madden explains that as coach he told his players repeatedly about the importance of enthusiasm – in fact, he advised his players that they must become "blind fanatics." He told the players he wanted to see that wild look in their eye – the kind that is classic of Bears player Mike Singletary. Madden says the players sometimes would take him at his word and "fling their bodies into the wedge on the kickoff with reckless abandon."

* * *

Madden shares an example of how the crowd can affect the team at halftime, "The visitor's locker room in War Memorial stadium was up a rickety wooden staircase. When you went out for the warm-up, you had to go down those stairs, and then past hotdog stands that were so close you could grab a mustard jar. Dozens of Bills fans were waiting to let you have it.

On the way back from the warm-up, and at halftime, you had to do it again. Every time, those fans were waiting for you."

* * *

Madden states that football is, "an emotional game." "Sure, football has to be played emotionally," he says. "And your players better play it that way. But in order to perform emotionally, a player must be prepared mentally. If he doesn't know which guy to block or which guy to cover, emotion isn't going to do him any good." Madden says, "hooting and hollering are kid stuff." "Just because players come charging out of their locker room whooping and hollering doesn't mean they are emotionally up," Madden says. "Some high school and college kids get more contact when they jump up and down and pound each other just after halftime than they get in the entire game."

* * *

"Whatever the coach tells them in the locker room must carry them through to the fourth quarter", Madden says, "because, that is where tough games are won or lost." It is then that I feel strongly that these guys need that energy to dig down deep and use the energy they saved by not whooping and hollering. In the pro locker room it is all about strategy.

They are always looking at the available photos taken from press box-level or higher – seeing the various coverages the opposing defense used. By halftime, all those photos have been separated into various down and distance situations – first down, second down, third down, short yardage, goal line, runs, passes, the different defensive fronts and pass coverage. I used a projector to enlarge the photos. I'd give out some new plays for the "next time situations."

* * *

In an interview appearing on the internet taken on the occasion of Madden being inducted into the Hall of Fame, David Humm a former player for Madden and had this to say about this colorful coach: "As far as a guy that can motivate I've never run into anybody like John Madden. He could give pre-game speeches and halftime speeches and he would rip you at practice to the point that he was so good at it you would just go "Man, that was good!" He was one that could just light up a locker room and light up the guys. He could rip you and then put his arm around you and he was an incredible motivator bringing the team together. You can see it on TV with his humor.

My rookie year we were 3-0 and we were going to play the Chiefs and they were 0-3 and we were like 30 point favorites. At halftime the Chiefs were beating us 42-0. Back in the Midwest in Kansas City it was hot and humid. That's when they had the chief on the horse and every time they scored this poor horse was doing laps around the field and by halftime this horse was so lathered up there was lather flying all over.

The chief had his headpiece off to the side and we go into the locker room and Madden doesn't come in. Everyone was sitting around and we were doing our meetings in groups and right at the end of halftime Madden walks in and calls us all up. Usually he gives us a speech to fire us all up for the second half. He said "Men, you've got to stop them. You're killing their horse!" and he walked out. We're all sitting there looking around and knowing we're getting killed and know we shouldn't laugh. It was one of the funniest lines I have ever heard. We were sitting there in a game situation and he did that one liner, turned and walked out."

* * *

Lester Hayes a cornerback for the Raiders, 1977-86 reminisces about Madden: "There are men who can speak to you on Sunday mornings and your pulse rate rises. That's a very unique gift coach Madden had. The pre-game speeches were so powerful I thought I could run through a brick wall. ... He would speak about war, and it would sound so good I thought I was listening to the second coming of General George S. Patton. It was like that every week. Coach Madden could speak to us in such a positive fashion; we thought we could not be beaten."

"I do not believe in failure—only results! If I can change what I do, I can always get a different result. Some of the greatest miracles of my life have not come by grand events—but rather by the little things I have chosen to do...every day."

Art Berg

9

Coach Frank Beamer on:
Halftime Coaching and Life

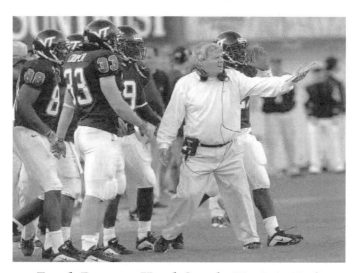

Frank Beamer, Head Coach, Virginia Tech

Frank Beamer is the head coach of Virginia Tech. He is known to be one of the most respected and notably inspirational football coaches in America. AP Sportswriter Jim Litke writes about the hidden story of Coach Beamer in an article titled, "The Determination Still Simmers: Know About His Inner Character And Background.

Frank Beamer's pathway to becoming a head coach at an esteemed university included some significant moments where he had to make important decisions about football and his life.

Beamer Background

Jim Litke relates: Early in his life story before football, Frank Beamer was lying flat on his back undergoing 30 operations just to keep going. He went into his personal "halftime" struggling, and came out working passionately to achieve his goals of playing football, overcoming adversity and conquering his challenges with personal victory. One could easily say, that the most revealing story about Frank Beamer has nothing to do with football.

It was 1954, long before Virginia Tech's coach had any idea how he would make his living or that one day he would play for a national championship. A long scar running down the right side of Beamer's neck is a reminder of that episode. Yet somehow, it wasn't until the spotlight landed on him that his own son learned the details. "He didn't like to talk about it," said Shane Beamer, who doubled as the long snapper for the Hokies, "and I didn't want to ask." It isn't hard to understand why.

Frank Beamer was an easygoing 7-year-old growing up on a farm in the tiny town of Fancy Gap, Virginia, passageway between two Appalachian peaks. One day, after helping his father burn a pile of trash, Frank carried a smoldering broom back into the garage. It ignited a can of gasoline, causing an explosion that left him with severe burns on the right side of his neck, shoulder and chest. Beamer's older brother, Barnett, probably saved his life. He had the presence of mind to roll Frank in the dirt and extinguish the flames. But the suffering was only beginning.

Over the next four years, Beamer underwent 30 operations, most of them skin grafts that didn't take. But every time he began to feel sorry for himself, Beamer's mother, an elementary school teacher, made him walk down the hall at the hospital. He always found someone in worse shape. Those memories steeled him for nearly every challenge that followed. "The doctors said he might be able to walk, but that he definitely was through with sports. He was determined to prove them wrong, and he did," Shane said. "If he tells you he's going to do something, whether it's golf or football or even cooking out, it will happen. I see that determination in him now more than anything." Beamer went on to play the games the doctors said he would not, and hasn't quit exceeding expectations since. He was a star quarterback in high school, and later, 5-foot-9, 170-pound starter at defensive back for Virginia Tech.

* * *

In the mid-1960s Beamer became the coach at Murray State. He then returned home to inherit a program that the NCAA had just put on probation. Beamer started in a rut and hit a handful of others on the way. He lost five of his first six games against rival Virginia. In his sixth year, he went 2-8-1 and learned that he wasn't the only one suffering the consequences. Shane and daughter Casey caught flak from schoolmates. Beamer's wife, Cheryl, heard about her husband's shortcomings in the grocery aisles. When the phone started ringing at home, it bothered Beamer more than the losses. If they wanted to write him, or call him, that's the way he wanted it to happen," Cheryl Beamer recalled. "I was naive. I thought everybody was nice. So I had our number listed." Coach Beamer has learned often in life that in order to play, you may have to overcome some tough circumstances.

* * *

COACH BEAMER ON HALFTIME
STRATEGY AND ACTIONS

(Interview with Don Grossnickle)

Coach, Can you call to mind a halftime moment or story that made a difference?

First: Screaming doesn't always get you very far.

In 1987, during my first year with Virginia Tech, the team traveled to New Orleans to play Tulane – a solid team going strong as it approached its seventh game of the season.

Meanwhile, with it being his first year, "we were struggling," he says,. "I recall we were playing lousy and they were playing great. The score was such that they were way ahead at halftime – we were being beaten pretty good."

Heading into the locker room, Tommy Groom, an older assistant coach with a lot more experience, stopped Beamer and told him point-blank: "Frank, you gotta jump all over these guys. We have to find a way to wake these guys up. You just got to go in there and pitch a fit."

Though Beamer acknowledges now – and did even then – that that wasn't really his normal approach, he figured Groom may have a point, especially given that his team's execution and even its effort were "sure as heck not very good," he recalls.

So, he took Groom's advice. He tore into the locker room screaming and hollering, throwing things and causing "a spectacle," he recalls. His final words to the awed team: "Guys, we need to get this thing right. If we aren't ready to come back out here and play better – don't even show up in the third quarter."

Within minutes of his parting words, Tulane's team ran Virginia Tech's second-half kickoff all the way into the end zone for a touchdown.

"So I guess my talk – they took me to heart: I think they didn't want to show up," chuckles Beamer now. "The one time I pitched a fit at halftime, and the opponent comes out and rolls right over us and scores a touchdown. "I look back and think that my time would have been much better spent getting some game plans worked out."

Coach Beamer: Do you think that emotion plays a key role in halftime?

If you have to force emotion into it, you probably aren't dealing with the right guys. "There are not many times since that day I just described, that I recall, that the boys have not given great effort," Beamer says. While there is certainly a time for emotion to come into play in the locker room, As a coach, you are much better off if you have good players that care about winning and the coach is much better off going in at halftime giving them some defensive schemes or offensive plays, or showing them how to block something that will make us better in the second half. Intense emotion – particularly the screaming and hollering – isn't usually worth it.

Have motivational tactics used by coaches at halftime changed much?

Things change. Change with them. It used to be that coaches could attack players with little worry. Today, for a coach that acts like that, he had better have his own lawyer sitting outside, because he is going to have a lawsuit.

When Beamer was a player, there were times that his coach might have asked me to run into a fence and I'd do it, he recalls. It's not that way anymore. The first question a player quickly asks: 'Why would you want me to run into that fence?' Things have changed. Today, he says, there hardly ever are times when things get loud. Instead, coaches talk about what individual players and the team can do in the second half to play better.

Do captains, team leaders and players ever play a role in halftime moments?

Others besides coaches can play key roles at halftime. There are plenty of times that players have spoken up at halftime, Beamer says.

Though he adds,: "I hope that if that happens, you get the right player to speak up. I have seen it where a guy would speak up and he is not the right one – he doesn't have the respect of his teammates." Of course, there are the ones who do have the respect, and when they demonstrate that they're ready to personally go back out and give every ounce of effort, "I think that would make a major difference."

Is there a central theme or style that guides you as a coach in leading at halftime:

The bigger it gets, the smaller you must think." That's one of Beamer's own quotes. Players and coaches don't go into the contest thinking about winning, he says. They must maintain their focus and zero in on the next play – and playing it the best that they can. All the attention has to be put into the effort for what you're doing right then. After that play is done, "get focused completely on the next play," Beamer advises. So many times, we get to thinking, 'Boy, we need to win this ball game' and 'What happens if we don't win this thing?' To Beamer, it comes back to his philosophy. The more complex the issue, the more you must focus in on the details. The bigger it gets, the smaller you must think.

What is the heart and soul of halftime?

As a coach, be who you are, handle what comes up and be consistent. From the early days of his coaching until now, Beamer has been consistent That's imperative, in his eyes. Because that way, the people he is in charge of know exactly what to expect, and know exactly what they're going to get. It is essential that the kids know that in any situation, they are going to get the same coach every time.

For him, that means focusing more on the technical aspects of the game, and what to do better to do better in the plays. Meanwhile, he likes his players to be consistent – that is, to want to win, to want to be successful and to be willing to put forth the effort to do both.

"Optimism is the faith that leads to achievement. Nothing can be done without hope and confidence."

Helen Keller

10

Bill Cowher: Halftime Relies On Teamwork

Bill Cowher
Head Coach Pittsburgh Steelers

(Interview with Don Grossnickle)

Coach Cowher: Can you describe a noteworthy halftime moment in the locker room?

Two years ago, we were playing the Cincinnati Bengals at home.

This was the same Sunday that the President declared that we were going to war and informed the American people that we had started to bomb. This world event put a lot of things in perspective at halftime – things like sticking together as a team.

Themes came to mind, like: We need to be one. We need to pull together. We need to be a family while our nation is going through this time. I used these themes and tried to communicate that we all needed to pull together to make things work.

I used the moment to get the feel for our game and game plan, and maintain focus – keeping the central things in perspective while still considering the bigger picture.

Another story comes from 1996 when we were trailing 10-6 in the first half playing the Minnesota Vikings. Our opponent was kicking a field goal in the final seconds. The Vikings ended up missing the field goal, but there was a flag down and the officials said we had twelve men on the field. I went around counting and even got a photo later on. I called time-out and told the officials we did not have twelve men on the field – and said I had a photo to verify it.

The officials didn't change anything; the Vikings tried again and kicked the goal.

I went running up to the official at halftime and stuck the photo in his pocket. Our team went into the locker room that day furious. We'd just been robbed of three points.

It was then that I gave what I think is one of my greatest of all time halftime speeches. I felt confident we were going to use this situation to our advantage.

This was going to provide motivation, I told my team. Our opponents think they are just going to get this gift; the officials just gave them 3 points. But we are going to come out in the second half and take control of this game.

As it turns out, we turned the ball over almost immediately in the third quarter.

The Vikings recovered a fumble for a touchdown. They had an interception returned for a touchdown, and they cumulatively scored 24 unanswered points.

Despite the fact that I though I had given one of my all-time great motivational halftime speeches, all it did was produce 24 points for the Vikings.

The final outcome of the game: They won, 44-24.

I took that speech and canned it and said to myself, "I am never going down that alley again." This goes to show that sometimes the greatest speeches have very little effect. In reality, it's not so much what a coach says – but how you play – that makes a difference.

Is there a slogan or theme that gets to your heart and soul at halftime?

I always think a lot about perspective.

I use it in reflecting and telling our players that in our profession, as much as we're scrutinized, "you are never as good as you think you are, and you are never as bad as they say you are." The point: When it's going well, don't take yourself too seriously. When it's going poorly, it's never as bad as it seems.

You can always get better. This is a great way of looking at life. When you are involved in sports, and involved with all the highs and lows, you have to possess the ability to keep things in perspective. Otherwise, you can let the emotional element of any sport drain you.

It is hard to sustain anything at any consistent level. This is one of the biggest obstacles for anybody who participates in sports and has to deal with the success and the adversity. You have to have the perspective to handle all the criticism while at the same time never really believing all the accolades they throw on you.

Halftime is a time to put things in perspective. Sometimes there is so much momentum involved in football games. The most important thing at halftime is to clear the mind. Clear the mind. Don't get involved with what just took place, because now it's time to start over again. You have to recapture your momentum.

A major role of the head coach is to find a way to swing the momentum back to your side. The first couple minutes of the second half are critically important in re-establishing the tempo of a football game. The best way of starting the second half is clearing your mind from the first half. You make adjustments, the head coach lets the assistant coaches talk – and everyone talk – about what they need to do, and then we come together at the last moments. In that final minute or two we confirm that we have to go back out there regardless of the score. And the biggest thing you have to do right then is realize that, at that point, the score really is 0-0.

All you can control is what happens in these first second-half moments, because that will establish the tempo this game is taking on – the kind of identity it is taking on.

I can't stress it enough: it is essential for there to be a clearing of the mind.

Describe how halftime unfolds.

As I walk into the locker room, I realize that I only have 12 or 13 minutes.

We get into the locker room and the players are split; we have offense on one side and defense on another side. We go into the coach's locker room and the coaches kind of gather their thoughts offensively and determine what we have to do: What are the adjustments we have to make? Here is what they are doing formation-wise; make sure we go over this. Here are the key adjustments we need to make right now. Here is what they are doing. This is what we have to do to adjust our game plan.

The job of the coaches is to convey all this. They meet quickly with their players up close. With about 2 minutes left before the second half, I call the players up and I kind of let them know where we are in the game plan. This is where we are. I explain that we have to do some better jobs on offense – taking care of the football; we have to get the ball in the second half, we have to re-establish the momentum, we have to get a score, we have to tackle better, we have to get them off the field on the third down. I lay out the things in that final speech in a nutshell. I tell them we're going to have to be smart … play smart … stay disciplined … stay focused.

For the coach's role, is halftime mostly a steady routine or do things vary?

I think halftime and coaching require a feel. It is not the same speech every halftime. It is not the same tone in my voice. I think that the head coach has to get a feel for what the team needs. If the team needs to be picked up and you feel you have some people starting to question things, you must respond by being positive. If you feel it is a team that needs to get a kick in the butt, then I respond.

I am going to come out and tell them the facts and the hard truth. The coach has to get a feel for the situation and realize that each game takes on its own personality – and, most importantly, the coach has to be himself. Nothing for me ever is premeditated. I do not have a premeditated talk. I am called upon to speak off the cuff. It is hard to say how it comes off and what the tone is.

I feel it's the coach's responsibility to make everyone aware of the realities of the given situation, to clarify the perspective and to emphasize the importance of finishing the job. I must make it clear that the team and players must take it one play at a time. Even if you're behind, We emphasize the importance of the play, not the scoreboard. The points on the scoreboard are taken care of when the play is done well.

"Before you can win a game, you have to not lose it."

Chuck Noll, former coach
Pittsburgh Steelers

11

Halftime Coaching
Wizardry and Magic

Successful head football coaches are called upon regularly to be magicians practicing their craft in the locker room. Every game, they're expected to know just what to do and just what to say. They incant just the right words and – presto-chango – all will be well in the second half … so long as everyone does their part.

We in the crowd – or we at home watching the game on television – want to know how they did it. We want to know what tools they used to inspire, what illusions they used to enliven courage and spark passion, what secret map helped them guide their team to the hidden treasure of a hard-won victory against a tough opponent.

But even if it is really magic – and many insist that it's not – do we really want to know about the secrets of halftime and the things coaches do to win? It is, after all, the mystery of what goes on behind the closed doors that makes it so intriguing. In the world of magic, telling secrets is optional and controversial. A good magician and perhaps great halftime football coaches take pride in the ability to perform, entertain and mystify. They perform their magic regardless of whether the audience ever knows how a trick is accomplished.

In this chapter we will take a close look at some of the tricks and gimmicks that coaches use to motivate and get the very best from the players and team as a whole. Here, we spill the beans on some of the master wizards of football.

Coach Gary Barnett

Coach Gary Barnett has taken motivational wizardry to the extreme. He is serious about the pursuit of motivation magic. He is passionate about finding and testing his motivational tools as any research scientist, and has a celebrated winning record to prove his effectiveness.

Barnett was named the 22nd head football coach in University of Colorado history in January 1999, after serving as head coach at Northwestern for seven years. In those seven seasons at Northwestern, his record included the outright Big Ten Conference title in 1995 and a shared championship in

1996. He took the Wildcats to their first bowl game in 47 years when the '95 team played USC in the Rose Bowl. His 1996 squad went to the Citrus Bowl, marking the first time Northwestern ever went bowling in back-to-back seasons. In the three decades before, the school had logged only two other winning seasons. Barnett frequently shares his insights about the importance of knowing and applying strategies that can impact players' emotion and attitude.

Notes from Barnett's Book-
<u>High Hopes-Taking the Purple to Pasadena</u>

A *textbook* of football coaching and motivational wizardry is found in Barnett's fascinating story, <u>"High Hopes – Taking the Purple to Pasadena."</u> Barnett's book (written with Vahe Gregorian) details many of the classic tools and tricks he used in getting a previously fledging team to the Rose Bowl. Barnett illustrates the dept of thinking and preparation many coaches put into their motivation and inspirational parts of the game and their coaching.

Barnett's wife is a big fan and admirer of his ability to motivate: "Gary has a special way of motivating and encouraging people (myself included) to find the inner strength, will, and determination to succeed," she says, "With this confidence comes the ability to accomplish great things. Gary has the uncanny ability to teach complex ideas through the use of concrete and visual stories. A gifted storyteller, he creates an inspiring and motivating vision that everyone can take home."

Barnett relates, "motivation can get sticky, because you're usually dealing with a large audience and all individuals are motivated differently. You have to have a feel for who responds to what, and when you're in a group setting it's hard to always know the right dynamic."

* * *

BARNETT'S ARSENAL OF MOTIVATIONAL WEAPONS

Gary Barnett's creativity when it comes to motivation is stellar. The following motivational tools are described throughout his book, <u>High Hopes-Taking the Purple to Pasadena.</u>

Creating a Clear Visual of Goals

During spring practice in 1995, Barnett held up a picture of a Velociraptor from the movie "Jurassic Park" and told his men, "This is what happened this spring: A baby Velociraptor has just broken through its egg. We have three months for it to grow up it into this...."

* * *

Turning a Program Around

Barnett relates more than once his analogy for creating an environment where people can find a way to accomplish expectations instead of automatically saying no. The closest analogy I have for our situation is a jigsaw puzzle," Barnett says. "When you buy a jigsaw puzzle, the only way you know what that puzzle is supposed to look like is by looking at the picture on top of the box – the vision of what the puzzle should ultimately be. When you open the box the only thing you see is chaos. A jigsaw represents a system for turning chaos into order. I had to figure out the vision of what that completed puzzle would be like. On January 11, 1992, at a crowded Northwestern basketball game, I was introduced to the student body. I was given the microphone and blurted out: 'We're going to take the Purple to Pasadena – to the Rose Bowl.' I was like Cortez when he conquered Mexico. He left no way out for his men – he burned the boats and there was no turning back. We hung a Rose Bowl banner in our locker room area. I put a rose in my office. I put a 1949 Rose Bowl ticket on display on my desk and put up a 1949 Rose Bowl poster. I sent out pieces of a jigsaw puzzle to new recruits.

* * *

Commitment

In football the most important factors in how good somebody can be lies in the heart and the decisions that are made about commitment," Barnett says. He relates this story: There is a story about a boy who goes to the zoo and sees a man selling balloons. The man has some helium balloons and some regular balloons. The kid sees a red balloon slip away from the man, and it goes straight up in the sky. Then the guy lets go of a green balloon and it just sort of falls to the ground and bounces around. So the kid says, 'Mister I want a red balloon,' and the man says, 'Why a red one?' 'Because it's the one that goes up in the sky,' the boy says. The man says, 'No, no – it's not the color of the balloon; it's what's inside the balloon that matters.' I explained to the players that all the things needed to be physically prepared – but to measure up to the opponents, I asserted, that must be because of a decision you made, or something inside of you! Man will do so much for a dollar, and more for another man – but he'll die for a cause. A cause is the glue that binds the jigsaw of life together, the blood that surges through it to bring it to life."

* * *

Bringing in Experts

In 1993, Barnett invited 71-year-old veteran coach Steve Musseau to camp. Musseau had been a head coach at the University of Idaho, and taught players and coaches how the mind works. How we think, how we learn, how we store things. His greatest lesson:, vividly imagined events and activities actually can be more productive than physically practiced ones, because anything vividly imagined becomes the truth in your mind. "Musseau was theatrical," Barnett recalls. "One time at a preseason meeting in 1995, I stood before the players and in walks a man tapping a cane and wearing a long wig, long robe and sandals. The players saw me respond with my mouth standing wide open and the players burst out in laughter. It took them a few seconds to realize who it was, but the guys who had been there two or three years knew, so I said, 'Coach Musseau?' And he answered, 'No, Moses!' I said, 'Moses?' He said, 'That's right, I've been lost in the desert since 1971, and I'm damned tired of it and I'm here to lead us out."

"Steve went into an oration about 'belief without evidence' and then put in a tape recording of Frank Sinatra singing 'High Hopes.' After a time, the guys began singing their lungs out whenever they heard this song – and for the 19 days of preseason, we had all kinds of dances and gestures and a rap mix to it. The song gave the team a theme and a value to strive for; high hopes. The goal was to beat Notre Dame in the first game."

* * *

Field Trip

"We took the players to the newly opened College Football Hall of Fame in South Bend on our way to play Notre Dame," Barnett says. "It was an incredible adventure for the players and coaches. There was an exhibit of a replica of a locker room with coaches giving speeches. The tour gave us a deep uplifted feeling, almost a tingle. We left there pretty jacked up and went on to beat them 17-15."

* * *

Inspiration

One of Northwestern's defensive backs, Marcell Price, was killed in a shooting in the summer of 1995. The team wore his nickname, "Big Six," on patches on our jerseys all season. We took his jersey with us to every game and hung it up before the kids walked out of the locker room". In every meeting we had before the game, I'd ask for the kids to play one play for Marcel. I told them I didn't care when they did it, but if they were in there on the field, I wanted them to pick one play for Marcel and bring him with us.

* * *

Focus and Concentrated Effort

Barnett explains how, in 1995, he always approached goals with more than just the football field in mind because he didn't want to be about winning at all costs. "To overcome our many obstacles, the qualities of belief, trust, patience, caring, listening, hard work, and faith are necessary," he says. "They are all part of the puzzle, and we have to find a keen focus to know how to integrate them all. A picture comes to mind: When you walk across stones in a stream, you must concentrate on the stones – because the minute you look up to see what is passing by, you're going to slide in the water. You have to focus on the stones and precisely where your feet are going.

* * *

Object Lesson

To illustrate a major point before a game, I took a ping pong ball and pushed it into a large jar of pinto beans. As I pushed the ball down into the beans, I said, 'There are going to be things out there that are going to get you down. There are going to be plays when you don't feel like getting back up, but you know what?' – And I would shake the jar and the ball would rise a little – "If you keep picking yourself up, about the fourth quarter, you're going to pick yourself up and win the game."

Magic

"At a magic store, I found one of those pitchers that look empty when it's been filled with water. Our colors were blue and white so I put blue water in it. "Before a game, I told the team, 'There are going to be times when you don't think there's anything left to give. You're going to want to give up.' Then, from an apparently empty pitcher, I'd pour a little water out and say, 'But if you reach down inside yourself and believe in yourself, there's always more.' "Then I poured more water out, drank it down and threw the glass against the shower room wall. It shattered – and there's just something about the sound of shattering glass that fires you up."

* * *

Intensity

In 1991, we were playing Purdue at their place. I broke the blackboard at our team meeting before we went on the field. I knew I was going to pound it, although I didn't necessarily plan on breaking it. "Purdue billed us for it. It was worth it. I was just reaching, trying to get the kids excited. We won 28-14 and I was pleased that our kids were happy but not obnoxious.

* * *

T-Shirts

The Chicago Sun-Times got on the bandwagon when we were going through a tremendous winning streak. They had thousands of T-shirts printed up that said on the front,

'Do you believe in miracles?' I got hold of some of them and had an additional slogan printed on the backside for the players that said: 'This Was No Damn Miracle.'

* * *

Tests

To place things in full perspective, there are motivational tactics Barnett uses to supplement the essential ingredient for coaching and winning: preparedness. "The usual routine prior to a game is to practice on Friday and then have meetings and give video tests," Barnett says. "The kids have to perform under the gun for offensive and defensive schemes. We walk through an image of a given play and every guy, one by one, calls out his assignment. This is part of the motivation to hold everyone accountable for our game plan."

* * *

According to outstanding coaches like Barnett, winning at football requires some thoughtful engineering to complement winning attitude and motivation. "In football, the most important factors in how good somebody can be lie in the heart and the decisions that are made about commitment." One of Barnett's mentors, the late Vince Lombardi, is credited with pointing him in the right direction – encouraging him to place proper focus and attention on learning to be a master motivator. Lombardi said: "Some guys play with their heads. That's okay. You've got to be smart to be number one in any business. But more important, you have got to play with your heart – with every fiber of your body. If you're lucky enough to find a guy with a lot of head and a lot of heart, he's never going to come off the field second."

"Never tell people how to do things. Tell them what to do and they will surprise you with their ingenuity."

George S. Patton

12

Superbowl:
The Ultimate Halftime

This chapter was written by sportswriter, Vic Carucci as he examines halftime at the Superbowl, perhaps the ultimate venue where professional athletes and coaches apply their wizardry.

(Reprinted by permission from Postseason issue of NFL Insider: Superbowl Program, 2003)

Halftime long has been a perfect setting for football drama. If a coach is unhappy with his team's showing through the first 30 minutes – or just wants to make sure it doesn't lose its edge – he can work his players into a wild frenzy with an inspirational speech. He might even punctuate his remarks by flipping a table or smashing a water cooler.

Even coaches not known for fiery temperaments have had memorable halftime tirades. In 1987, as defensive coordinator of the San Francisco 49ers, George Seifert, kicked a chalkboard leaning against a cement wall so hard, he broke his toe. And that was while the 49ers held a 20-0 lead. In 1989, Joe Gibbs, then the coach of the Washington Redskins, took out his frustrations by trashing a tray of oranges.

But neither incident happened during halftime of a Super Bowl, which Seifert and Gibbs each have won as head coaches.

Given the game's magnitude, one would expect the atmosphere to be ripe for the sort of fireworks that the rest of the stadium and millions of television viewers get to watch after the teams disappear into the tunnel. It isn't. Halftime in a Super Bowl locker room is far more clinical than emotional. It is a time for rest. It is a time for reflection. It is a time for review. It is a time for refocusing.

"It might happen once in a season where you have to get emotional at halftime because players aren't playing real hard," two-time Super Bowl-champion coach Mike Shanahan says. "If anything, during the Super Bowl you want to go in the other direction. You want a calming atmosphere because the players are jacked anyhow. They know how important it is, so if anything, you've got to approach it more that this is another game."

"The players have been put through a wringer all week and through the first half," says Pro Football Hall of Fame coach Marv Levy, who directed the Buffalo Bills to four consecutive Super Bowls. "Almost the last thing you need at halftime is some contrived pep talk."

Still, there is plenty of time for one, if not an entire lecture series. For regular-season games, halftime lasts 12 minutes. To accommodate the major production of a Super Bowl halftime show, intermission lasts at least twice as long. As a semi-serious Shanahan points out, it is long enough to "put in a whole new game plan." Of course, he never had the urge to do so because his Denver Broncos were ahead at intermission in both of their Super Bowl victories (against Green Bay in Superbowl XXXII and Atlanta in XXXIII).

The greatest challenge for every Super Bowl coach is to use the extra time wisely. Coaches have the ability to cover far more strategic ground than they normally can at halftime, but they have to be mindful of not dispensing more information than can be absorbed and careful not to allow too much anxiety or, worse, boredom to set in.

After being hastily herded off the field to make room for the massive stage and other set-up work for the halftime show, players follow their usual routine. They head for their dressing cubicles to take a seat and to catch their breath. They refuel by grabbing an orange or two and a cold bottle of water or a sports drink. There is time for restroom stops, visits to the trainers, and equipment repair.

Bill Walsh, who coached the 49ers to three Super Bowl victories, always insisted his players take about 10 minutes just to relax before being hammered with the inevitable barrage of coaching points.

"It's important not to just sit there the whole time and get cold," says Denver receiver Ed McCaffrey, who won two Super Bowl rings with the Broncos and one with the 49ers. "You're sitting down for about a half-hour, so you have to make sure you stay loose, ready to go. You just kind of keep moving. I like to take maybe ten to fifteen minutes of rest, and then kind of move around, stretch, and make sure I'm ready to go when we go back to the field."

The assistant coaches who are stationed in the press box leave for the locker room before the end of the half. As soon as they arrive, they use grease boards in the middle of the room to illustrate various offensive and defensive schemes by the opponent. The illustrations are complemented with still photographs showing how the plays unfolded.

"You spend a whole week looking at a playbook, and then you get on the field and things are different," former Bills center Kent Hull says. "That grease board is going to be the playbook now for the second half." The players are divided by units – offense on one side, defense on the other – and the locker room becomes a classroom. The head coach and coordinators talk about what the team did in the first half, how the opponent attacked it, and the necessary adjustments for the final two quarters. After that, players gather with their position coaches for more detailed sessions.

"Instead of coming in and getting a couple of instructions on the board in ten minutes and going right back out there, you're going to have twenty to thirty minutes," says tight end Shannon Sharpe, who won two Super Bowl rings with the Broncos and one with the Baltimore Ravens. "So, basically, you get an opportunity to sit down, listen, and talk."

Still, the words uttered and strategic decisions made at some halftimes live on:

Superbowl XIV: Trailing the Los Angeles Rams 13-10, the Pittsburgh Steelers were unhappy with the performance of their vaunted defense, even though it had allowed only 1 touchdown and 2 field goals. "How can you mess up this way?" assistant coach Woody Widenhofer told the defensive unit. "Didn't we go over these things a dozen times? You guys are standing out there like statues." The Steelers gave up only 6 more points on the way to a 31-19 victory, their fourth triumph in as many Super Bowls.

Superbowl XXI: Trailing Denver 10-9, New York Giants coach, Bill Parcells, was dissatisfied with the results of an aggressive offensive game plan – his team had passed 9 times and run only twice on first down. He thought it was "too helter-skelter," and ordered that the Giants go back to their basic approach of Joe Morris running the ball and Phil Simms throwing off play-action to tight end Mark Bavaro. Simms went 10 for 10 in the second half, and the Giants won 39-20.

Superbowl XXIII: Tied with the Cincinnati Bengals 3-3, Walsh and the 49ers' offensive coaches decided that their biggest headache was the dominant play of Bengals safety David Fulcher. The solution, use two tight ends to reduce the effectiveness of his blitzing, and start running away from him. The outcome: a 20-16 San Francisco victory decided by Joe Montana's unforgettable 92-yard drive in the final 3:10.

Superbowl XXVIII: Trailing the Bills 13-6, the Dallas Cowboys knew changes were in order, especially on offense. Emmitt Smith, who ran for 41 yards in the first half, wanted to take over the game. "Get me the ball!" Smith told offensive coordinator Norv Turner, who later admitted that in an effort to establish more offensive balance with his play calling, he "was forcing some passes that really weren't there." Smith finished with 132 rushing yards and was the most valuable player in the Cowboys' 30-13 victory.

Once the Xs and Os are sorted out, the head coach will address the entire squad, usually to establish a theme for the second half. For instance, with his Redskins trailing the Miami Dolphins 17-10 in Super Bowl XVII, Gibbs reminded his players that they had rallied from larger deficits to win and that he was certain they would do it again. They did, winning 27-17.

Then there was this surprisingly concise summary from loquacious Ravens coach Brian Billick after his team built a 10-0 halftime lead over the Giants in Super Bowl XXXV: "If we don't turn the ball over, we're world champs." They didn't, and they were, rolling to a 34-7 triumph.

Players will chime in with words of inspiration for their teammates. Then, there's a knock on the door. The referee gives a three-minute warning before both teams are to return to the field. There have been times when the warning has been premature, and players have ended up charging down the tunnel, only to be held back until all of the people and apparatus from the halftime show were cleared. In order to avoid that, Walsh assigned someone from the 49ers' support staff to verify when the time was right to leave the locker room. The last thing players want after a lengthy halftime in the biggest game is to hurry up – and wait. "Either you're sequestered or you're on the field," Walsh says. "You don't want to run a team through a crew that's moving a big stage or have them standing around while the fireworks are still coming down."

"Sometimes you hear the show, and you know, obviously, it's something big," Hull says. "But for the most part I don't think you're even cognizant of what's happening."

For players and coaches in a Super Bowl, the only halftime activity that matters takes place in the locker room. To sum things up, football halftime can be thought of being possibly reduced to a simple whimsical formula: equal parts cerebral and equal parts emotion, all played out on an imaginary chessboard. So much of football hinges on attitude.

"Leaders aren't born, they are made. And they are made just like anything else, through hard work. And that's the price we'll have to pay to achieve that goal, or any goal."

Vince Lombardi

13

Competitive Leadership: Halftime and More

Brian Billick, Baltimore Ravens

Two-thirds of the teams in the NFL have changed head coaches just in the two years since I was hired to coach the Baltimore Ravens. In the halftime part of the game, in fact in any part of the game, or in life for that matter – you must be able to adapt to whatever profile your players' assets dictate. While you should have a determined and consistent approach philosophically to the way you plan to operate your team, it had better include a level of anticipatory flexibility that enables you to adapt to your changing circumstances as needed.

The great leader, Winston Churchill, spoke about the imperative of a leader mastering both the "tricks of the trade" along with a solid foundation of skillfulness when he said, "The genius of a great leader consists in the constant harmony of holding a variety of great purposes in mind all at once." This statement applies to the role of the coach – especially at halftime. As a leader, your goals and aspirations must be strong enough to sustain you through the toughest of times.

Trust me, if your goals are set high enough and your aspirations are worthy enough, there will be tough times. In the NFL, there are 32 head football coaches – each with a diverse set of individual attributes and personal characteristics. Each possesses a tremendous passion for what he does. The common denominator is their passion for the game.

I have to be on guard so that my emotions do not override my judgment. A basic task of the competitive leader is to develop a balance between passion and accountability. Anything worth doing is seldom achieved without passion. As our 26th president Theodore Roosevelt once noted, "Far and away, the best prize that life offers is the chance to work hard at work worth doing." Passion is the lubricant of success.

A new paradigm of leadership is to create a vision for the organization and realize the responsibility for motivating and inspiring others in the pursuit of greater goals than they might have believed possible. This is the essence of competitive leadership. No single itemized recipe exists for leadership – especially for locker room leadership.

The mix of the traits and qualities required to lead successfully in a given situation tends to vary from situation to situation and from individual to individual. Locker room leadership goes beyond the passion, emotions and desire of the moment.

In almost every human endeavor, the more you can prepare and the greater the effort you expend, the more likely you will be successful.

My father was a test pilot. He frequently spoke of the value of maintaining an established routine to insure that you did not "miss a step" in the heat of the moment. He often told me that living with an established well-thought-out structure was always your best chance to survive.

Good luck possibly helps win games, but preparation absolutely predicts success. The great coaches of the NFL today attend to detail and innovation. Very specific attention is given to situational, contingency and reactive needs of each of our teams by a process that is designed to maintain the learning curve of the players.

Coaches are responsible for conditioning and preparing the players for every possible contingency that they might face in a game situation. By taking this approach, coaches can reduce the level of uncertainty. Being well-prepared allows them to be aggressive and assertive to carry out their obligations in the game and meet emerging opportunities.

I do not attempt to trick my players with some pseudo-psychology. Loyalty is important – loyalty to our structure, our goals and each other. I try to make graphically clear to everyone that loyalty will sustain us through tough times. When the great teams in life are examined in sports, business, the military, politics and education, etc., it is abundantly clear that loyalty can be an exceptional catalyst for inspired performance.

Skillful leaders in the halftime locker room – or at any time – not only inspire genuine loyalty toward them, but also extend a demonstrable level of loyalty toward those that follow them. One of the most essential duties of a skillful leader is to be a motivator. An important way that leaders can enhance motivational levels in the organization is to cultivate an environment of motivation within the workplace.

In other words, the climate within the workplace should be such that it facilitates job performance. I really believe that perhaps the single most important action a leader can take to motivate individuals is to involve them fully in the steps that are taken to establish individual or group goals and responsibilities.

My ability to motivate emanates from several factors. I believe my fundamental knowledge of being able to set goals and establish directives will give the players the confidence and structure they need to be successful. I attempt to create a positive atmosphere that heightens the learning curve.

In the halftime locker room, I am called upon to be a problem solver. I am called upon to recognize a problem and solve it. Additionally, I am challenged to foresee and prevent problems before they occur. Each of these factors involves a certain degree of skill and systematic thinking. I can recall a time when I had to struggle with problem solving. In the 2000 season, we were in the throes of a three-game losing streak. We were standing at the edge of the abyss, and everyone knew it.

If all I had to offer my players at that time were a series of coaching clichés and a sense of false bravado, our players would have exposed my fraudulent efforts in the previous loss. This also was not a time to use pseudo-psychology to trick players into believing that they are somehow better than they actually are. It is in moments such as these that your confidence as a leader comes through in genuine fashion.

Oddly, a team on a losing streak may have some of the same properties of a winner. For example, both will tend to focus too much on the pressures they are enduring for the final consequences that the season might bring. In the process, they lose the level of critical focus needed.

Most teams on a losing streak tend to dwell on the negative factors that losing will cause, making the situation look even bleaker than it really is. By keeping the focus on the immediate task at hand (i.e. win a game and stop the slide), you can help your players overcome debilitating emotional reactions they might experience such as self-pity and hopelessness. Similar to a batter in a hitting slump, it takes a great deal of experience and inner confidence to know that this situation will ultimately pass. You should focus on whatever positives have occurred and continually show examples of how close they are to getting back on the right track.

The great coach John Wooden asked: "Why do we fear adversity when we know it is the only way to truly get better?" Adjusting at halftime is tricky. I particularly appreciate the anonymous quote, "The only thing wrong with doing nothing is that you never know when you are finished." Competent leaders have the sense and insight to avoid pursuing any quick fix that might hurt the organization in the long run. Coaches at halftime have to keep cool under pressure. Leaders who can respond to crises in an appropriate manner have to maintain their demeanor and inspire confidence in others by, as the saying goes, possessing the ability to keep their head while others around them are losing theirs. Coaches routinely are called upon to handle a crisis in a way that thoughtfully considers and evaluates the potential solutions from a broad perspective. A key feature of competitive leaders is that they are willing to modify their strategy as needed whenever the circumstances dictate such a change is justified.

Halftime leaders are called upon to possess the ability to act quickly and decisively. Given the urgent nature of a crisis, there is time to conduct lengthy investigations into what possible solutions might ultimately help alleviate the crisis. Accordingly, the coach-leader must learn to trust his intuition and to consider his gut feelings as one factor in developing and evaluating potential solutions.

On the morning after winning Superbowl XXV, I couldn't help but think back to the sequence of events that had formed and defined the personality of my organization, my team and indeed the very fabric of my abilities as a head coach in the National Football League. We had identified our problems, developed a solution and moved beyond any indecision, and now, because of our cumulative strengths and loyalties, the victory was ours. Challenges in training, in game situations and in life prove to be a significant catalyst and an integral part of the backbone that helps create our success. Looking back, I have made the observation that the fundamentals and approach to the game of football haven't changed a great deal in the last 70 years or so since the exemplary coach Knute Rockne was making history and establishing lore and legends.

The basic concepts are timeless, and the fact remains that football is essentially a game of numbers and angles. As a coach, you have to bring superior numbers to the point of attack – and if you can't do that, you have to supply superior angles for your athletes in a one-on-one match up. Teamwork and team spirit are fostered when a leader takes specific steps to enable groups to lead themselves. The head coach must sometimes pull back even a step farther than his coordinators. He must have the broadest perspective of all. The coach must inspire courage. Physical courage is courage in the face of personal danger, while moral courage is courage of responsibility to others or to a purpose.

If one's resolve is based on one's own commitment to the team and the team's ultimate achievements, then one can hold up against the strongest of attacks because your convictions are genuine. Above all else, that is the greatest gift I have received from winning a championship. Coaches at halftime must possess self-confidence. Self-confidence enhances the ability of leaders to conquer adversity, such as setbacks, disappointments, and embarrassments. Almost every leader will have to deal with at least one significant setback in their career. The more capable they are of handling negative circumstances, the better able they will be to bounce back from most any situation. Halftime is a special aspect of the game. It offers time to reflect and sort things out. As I stood atop the podium in Tampa with the Lombardi Trophy firmly in hand, I recognized that I had reached the top of superstar Coach John Wooden's well-known pyramid and realized the value of the top tier of competitive greatness. I had self-actualized the line from the movie, <u>The Legend of Baggar Vance:</u> *"You can never win this game. All you can do is play it."*

"Winning is not a sometime thing;
it's an all time thing. You don't win once
in a while, you don't do things right once
in a while, you do them right all the time.
Winning is habit. Unfortunately, so is
losing."

Vince Lombardi

14

Classic Fire Breathing Halftime Coaches and Quotes

Knute Rockne

The legendary Knute Rockne of Notre Dame Football fame is credited with being the grand master of football inspirational oratory. It is said, no one could light the fire, no one could unleash the passion, and no coach possessed the ability of Rockne to turn the tables at halftime and send the team out to accomplish extraordinary feats. In his too-short life and career, Rockne built a reputation for his skillfulness in manipulating the human spirit that surprised everyone, perhaps, on occasion, even him. Rockne died in a plane crash in 1931 at the age of 43, yet his speeches and inspiring quotes abound in locker rooms, boardrooms and wherever the importance of human attitude is celebrated. Rockne believed in the catalytic power of attitude and motivation.

* * *

Rockne biographer Bill Bilinski writes in The Sporting News College Football's Twenty-Five Greatest Teams: "Football was a game of emotion for Rockne. Knute Rockne once said that, "football is a game of wit and intelligence, not brute strength. Rockne knew how to use it to his advantage. His famous locker room speeches tapped his players' emotions, giving the Irish the motivational edge they sometimes needed to win. He was effervescent and he was quite an actor. He could really get you worked up. We never went into a game flat. Even if it meant telling a white lie to inspire his troops, Rockne did what it took. For example, one time Rockne thought his squad needed a shot in the arm to beat a superior Georgia Tech team in Atlanta in 1922 when the famous "Four Horsemen " were sophomores. Coach Rockne broke into tears before the game when he read a telegram to the team about the serious illness of his son, Billy. The players made it their mission to win for little Billy, They succeeded, getting pretty banged up in the process and returned triumphantly to South Bend where one of the first fans to greet the team was, you guessed it, Billy Rockne. Not only did the players win the game, but they effected a miraculous cure in the process."

* * *

In 1999, The Sporting News listed Rockne 76th among the 100 most important people in this century's sports world, calling him "football's greatest motivator." How did he discover the hidden secrets of inspiring attitude and motivation? What were his thoughts about attitude and football? Why are his speeches used as a model for students of persuasive rhetoric? Listen to the fire of Rockne in one of his well known speeches:

"We're going inside of 'em, we're going outside of 'em – inside of 'em! outside of 'em! – and when we get them on the run once, we're going to keep 'em on the run. And we're not going to pass unless their secondary comes up too close. But don't forget, men – we're gonna get 'em on the run, we're gonna go, go, go, go! – and we aren't going to stop until we go over that goal line! And don't forget, men – today is the day we're gonna win. They can't lick us – and that's how it goes ... The first platoon men – go in there and fight, fight, fight, fight, fight! What do you say, men!"

* * *

Rockne emphatically told everyone his views on the importance of attitude and mental habits when it came to football. Rockne said, "The freak psychologists will tell you that a shot of adrenaline will cure cowardice in the case of a football player who is afraid. The practical football coach knows that this is a lot of bunk. He knows that if a man is yellow, he is yellow, whereas the boy with character and willpower will overcome his fears and will go into the game showing those qualities we know as raw courage. Courage is largely a matter of breeding, environment, and the development of the proper mental habits."

Here is one version of the classic Rockne legendary halftime episode: "One time they were trailing by half time, going into the locker room completely demoralized and dreading the speech Rockne was sure to deliver, but he wasn't there. "The team waited; no Rockne. Time passed; still no Rockne. The umpire called ,"5 minutes left," and there was still no Rockne. The umpire called "2 minutes left," and suddenly Rockne burst through the door and, with scorn dripping from his lips, said: "Fighting Irish." Then he spat, turned on his heel and stalked out the door. "One of the guys on the team exclaimed, "Well, what are we waiting for?" and, with a roar, the team ran back out on the field and they tore the other team apart and won the game.

Rockne's attitudes about motivation remain alive today. He inspired one of the classic American films about the game of football, and the famous, "Win One for the Gipper Speech" is indelibly marked into the memories of those who saw that halftime locker room scene, heard the speech in person or read it in print. The "Win One for the Gipper" speech was delivered to the Notre Dame players at halftime of the 1928 Army game.

Rockne was trying to salvage something from his worst season as a Notre Dame oach. To inspire the players, he told them the story of the tragic death of the greatest player ever at Notre Dame, George Gipp. Although historians believe it is doubtful that Rockne's version of Gipp's last words was true, Notre Dame did win that game against Army. More importantly, the story became solidified into popular culture after its re-creation in the 1940 movie "Knute Rockne – All American." And the phrase "Win one for the Gipper" was infused into the lexicon of American society, eventually becoming a rallying cry for the political campaigns of the actor who played Gipp in the movie: Ronald Reagan. Here's the transcript of the dialogue, from the MGM movie:

ROCKNE: Well, boys … I haven't a thing to say. Played a great game … all of you. Great game. I guess we just can't expect to win 'em all. I'm going to tell you something I've kept to myself for years – none of you ever knew George Gipp. It was long before your time. But you know what a tradition he is at Notre Dame … And the last thing he said to me – "Rock," he said, "Sometime, when the team is up against it and the breaks are beating the boys, tell them to go out there with all they've got and win just one for the Gipper" … "I don't know where I'll be then, Rock," he said, "but I'll know about it – and I'll be happy." There is a hushed stillness as Rockne and the crowd of boys look at each other. In the midst of this tense silence, Rockne quietly says "Alright," to the men beside him, and his chair is wheeled slowly out of the dressing room. PLAYER # 12 Well, what are we waiting for? With a single roar, the players throw off their blankets and rush through the doorway.

Actor Pat O'Brien About To Give A Rendition
Of The Ever Famous Locker Room Halftime Talk:
"Win One For The Gipper"
Notre Dame Vs Army 1928

Woody Hayes , Ohio State Buckeyes

Woody Hayes wrote in his book, <u>Hot Line to Victory</u> (retold in AFCA Football Coaching Strategies: "A good football squad is controlled better by attitudes than by rules. Attitude includes many things: First the desire to improve individually, to warrant membership on a team; second, the desire to win as translated into team conduct: and third, the development of a high respect for the rights and privileges of others on the squad.

* * *

According to former Ohio Sate player, Rex Kern, "Woody's pre-game talks were legendary. But they were scary at times. Coach Hayes always dwelt on military tactics and was probably always at his best pre-game, halftime, and his motivation to get players ready to play, prepared to play, were beyond compare. Once we completed our pre-game warm-ups, we would come back into the locker room and in Ohio Stadium we had this little old locker room downstairs that we would all go in, and each player, each position had a specific place where they sat.

The chalkboard and Coach Hayes would be front and center if you were walking in the room, and the quarterbacks would be off on the left. The offensive linemen were in the front row, and with the offensive centers and guards, and so on and so on. And Woody would have each player sit there, and there would kind of be silence in the room for a little while. And then occasionally Coach Hayes would come from around the side of the blackboard and down little, really a small corridor, but still within the locker room, and we, as underclassmen were always prepared our sophomore year,

"Hey, when Woody comes into the room, you don't say a word. Everybody shuts up, and you listen to Coach Hayes." Well, Woody would come in with some kind of a little story, strategically, to get us fired up and ready to play. But the main theme that Coach Hayes would always talk about is, "We always play hard. We play fair. We've worked hard. We'll out hit our opponents, and we'll never ever ever give up." He said, "the team that quits first, will be the team that'll lose, and by God that's not gonna be us," he would say, and he would go on and he would emphasize that.

Woody and Bo always thought that there was maybe some form of espionage going on in the locker room and here we are in our own stadium and Woody's whispering, "Ok, our first play…" And he looks around the room, and he's looking for hidden microphones, okay! He thinks that maybe the opponents have slid in a microphone. "…is gonna be, " and then he'd whisper. Or he would turn to the blackboard, and he'd write the play on the blackboard, and then he'd erase it real quick and get it real clean, so that nobody could see what the play was gonna be or that they would ever know.

It became more emphasized when we would play at a visiting team like that school up north or Minnesota, Wisconsin, some place like that. Woody was more careful because he thought, those opposing coaches, they're looking in my locker room and they know exactly what I'm saying. So you would kind of get a little bit of humor, but then you would obviously get caught up in it and you'd think, "oh yeah, shhh, we gotta be quiet and listen," because we want to make sure we know what the play is. But that would be kind of the atmosphere or the attitude of the locker room. It was very serene. It was very quiet. It was very attentive.

Woody would get all fired up and if he didn't think you were paying attention, he'd whack you on the shoulder pads and make sure that you were paying attention, and you know, "this is serious stuff, you know, this is what we've practiced for, this is what we've worked for"

There was always very strong meaning in, "we've got to do our best and never ever ever give up." And he said, "there are gonna be times out there that things won't go well for you." And he said, "Don't quit. Don't quit. Do not quit." And then he may launch off and say, "You know, in life, you don't quit, you don't ever ever quit." He said, "The great thing that football does for us is it teaches you that when you get knocked down, you get up quick. You can't lie down. You've gotta get up and get back into the game. If you don't, you're not any use to your football team, and if you don't get up in life, you're not any use to your civilization and to your community." And so, Woody would bring those things about. "

Earle Bruce , Ohio State Buckeyes

Woody Hayes', former assistant coach, Earle Bruce says. "I think in certain situations pep talks are important. "You give them when the team needs to be motivated; it comes with having a feeling. I was there at Minnesota when Woody put his fist through a plywood wall. We went back two years later and the hole was still there. All the kids were looking at it and so were we. You didn't want to be around if things were not going right. We stood back, way back. My belief is that players have a good memory. Once used, a specific pep talk cannot be given verbatim until the freshmen have graduated. You can reuse them if you change jobs, and every four years, but once a kid has heard a pep talk I don't know if it works on him," Bruce said. "You also have to remember the ones that work, and they work only if you win."

Coach Vince Lombardi, Green Bay Packers

Football coaching legend Vince Lombardi developed a reputation for his motivational charisma. Lombardi's style developed early in his career as evidenced in this description from a biographical sketch relating his halftime demeanor as a young assistant coach in a small Catholic high school in New Jersey. "Before the third game against Tenafly, Head Coach,

Palau, asked Lombardi to give the team a pep talk, and when it was over realized that his assistant had a fire inside that he could not match, "I knew he was intense about the game and I knew he got excited," Palau said later, "But that pep talk was incredible. I had never seen anything like it before. I was shaking in my boots when it was over, and I know the team was, too." Eyes bulging, eyelids blinking, fist clenched, Lombardi finished his speech, approached the starters one by one, said that they had done nothing to impress him during the practice that week and demanded more. "What are you going to do today?" He thundered. They went on to win 13-0 and Lombardi's team did not lose again that season."

Former Green Bay Packers center Bill Curry recalls just one halftime speech during his entire 10-year playing career. He was a rookie when the Packers, coached by the legendary Vince Lombardi, were getting handled by the Detroit Lions. The Lions had just returned an interception for a touchdown, adding to the Packers' misery. Both teams shared the same sideline, and as Lions lineman Alex Karras was exiting the field, he turned to Lombardi and screamed, "How'd you like that, you fat bleeping bleep?!" Curry expected Lombardi would criticize and berate his underachieving club at halftime. Instead, the coach stood alone through most of the intermission and said nothing. Just before the Packers returned to the field, Lombardi told his team, "Men, we are the Green Bay Packers," He then turned and calmly walked out. Green Bay won the game, crushing Detroit in the second half.

Coach Don Shula, Former Coach, Miami Dolphins

Just ask any veteran fan, professional player, or football coach about some of the most emotional personalities in the game. Soon, and without a doubt Coach Don Shula's name appears. His assistant coach, Monte Clark, once told the New York Times: "Don Shula is competitive in everything…. He's competitive eating breakfast." Writing about this charismatic motivator, his booming voice is said to leave scorch marks on the uniforms of his players when he is angry, and his belief in rigorous conditioning is every bit as strong as it was when he began his coaching career a quarter century ago. "If you win, it makes for an easier life," admitted Larry Csonka, Shula's former star running back, "because, if you lose, Shula goes crazy."

Coach Joe Paterno, Penn State Master Motivator

(Joe Paterno's Speech at the AFCA January 18, 2002) after being presented with the Amos Alonzo Stagg Award

Let me just talk about a couple of other things that I think are important – I won't keep you that long, I don't want to bore you. I think we all have to understand that football basically is a morale game. You play with your heart; you play with your mind. If you've got morale, then you've got a chance to win. If you've got the right kind of people, then you've got a chance to win. It is a morale game. At least, if you've got morale, then you have a chance to play as well as you can. No morale, no chances. I think morale is made up of two basic things. I think it's made up of pride, and I think it's made of loyalty. To me, I don't think pride is tough to get. My brother spent some time in the Marine Corps, he got out of the Marine Corps my dad was in the infantry, hated the Marines; absolutely hated them. My brother gets out of Brown with me and decides he's going to go into the Marine Corps. My dad gets all uptight and says, "I don't want a Marine in this house.' And George says, I don't want to go into the Army. I get seasick so I don't want to go into the Navy. I can be a Marine and in two years be an officer. He says, "Pop, relax. The Marines aren't that bad." "So, 17 weeks later, after basic training and boot camp, my brother comes home on a Saturday night. He got home at 11 o'clock on a Saturday night – it was great to see him, he looked good, he was in shape, the whole bit – came home in his uniform. My mother had pressed some clothes for him to go to church thinking he wasn't going to wear the darn uniform. He gets up in the morning and says he's going to wear his uniform. Now, my dad's eyes opened real wide and says, "Oh, he's going to wear his uniform? We've got to go to church with a Marine?'

So now we go to church, and in Brooklyn, my mother would cook all day Sunday, and we came home from Mass and everybody in the neighborhood – the kids would come in, my mom would feed us and my dad would open a bottle of wine and we'd sit around and shoot the bull. My dad was a great guy because if you said 'black,' he'd say 'white.' If you said 'Republican,' he'd say 'Democrat.' He loved to needle people, just loved to be involved, and he was just really a lot of fun to be around. So as soon as three or four of George's buddies get in there, he starts pecking away. "The Marines. bunch of patriots, right? They kill a mosquito, they want a medal."

(Laughter). My brother is sitting there, angry, and all of a sudden he jumps up and he walks over to my dad, and he says, "'Pop, knock it off. The Marines are the greatest fighting force ever put on the face of the Earth." I can still see my dad, Lord have mercy, he can't stop laughing. My dad is rolling on the floor because he cannot stop laughing. He got him because when he walked into that boot camp there, they said the greatest men in the world walked through those gates. Not some of the best, not pretty good, THE greatest walked through those gates. You've got to get up at 5 o'clock in the morning. Those shoes have got to look good. You better stand straight. You're a Marine! Look at all the Marines that went before you. Look at the tradition. In 17 weeks, they got it across to that kid. Just because you have the courage in you – you're willing to pay the price to be a Marine. That is a story of pride. To be a Penn State football player, or to be whatever you're involved in! It starts with morale and it is a matter of pride. If you start going down, reach down inside of you and find these ideals to hold on to."

Coach Bo Schembechler, University of Michigan Wolverines

Some people have often described the distinguished coach of the University of Michigan Wolverines as possibly the "meanest, toughest football coach that ever lived." Further, people have noted that he smashed headsets, kicked trash cans, whacked defensive linemen, screamed at quarterbacks, made referees cringe, turned sportswriters into jelly and had his players so frightened sometimes they forgot to breathe. "All that is true, Bo writes in his autobiography, "Life, Laughs, and Lessons of a college football legend:" There are a lot of ways to motivate football players. Sometimes you have to scare the crap out of them. Sometimes you have to lead by example. Sometimes you just have to get out of their way. And always, you have to keep up your act.

As a coach, I am the consummate actor. I am acting every minute of the day. Everything I say, every comment I make is designed with an effect in mind. I may walk by a player and bark at him, "I hope you're on your way to class." That's my subtle way of letting him know I've seen his midterm grades. I may yank aside a player during practice and holler, "Son, with your body and my brains I would have been unstoppable!" He knows that he better concentrate a little harder. "I may snarl. I may whisper. I may slap a guy on the back or yank him down by the face mask. It is all calculated. It is all designed for maximum effect. Acting: Always acting."

Bo defines motivation as, "quite simply, the spark that makes someone do that which he might not otherwise do. You need a ton of it in football. Let's be honest, it's unnatural for people to want to hit each other. You can't just tell a player, go out there and cream that guy because I told you to." Football he says "is a tough, bloody sport, with contact so fierce it can make you wince. If you expect your players to excel, you better have a pretty good reason, and that reason must be the pursuit of excellence. Not for the individual – for the team. You will never get the same level of effort from one man seeking glory as from a group of men pulling for a shared goal.

The secrets of motivation that Bo discovered:

1. You must know your players like a book. Know their personalities. Know what works.

2. You must be true to your own personality. There are some guys who can be very soft and say, 'I wish you had done

better,' and hurts some player's feelings. I'd probably say, 'Damn it, I'm going to kill you!'

3. Deep down, your players must know you care about them. This is the most important thing. I could never get away with what I do if the players felt I didn't care.

There are countless little things you to do motivate your team. Mostly, however, you talk. That is a coach's greatest motivational tool. That is what I work at the most. When I talk, I am passionate about the game. I may speak about Michigan, the school, the tradition. I may speak about the opponent and how little regard they have for us. I may speak about courage or pride. It depends. I never prepare a speech; whatever comes out comes out. For a big game like Ohio State or Michigan State, I might begin: 'Men, many others have played in this game before us. Tradition demands that you play like Michigan! That is why you're here! You did not come to play in a mediocre program, and if you did, you are in the wrong place. … "The words come from the heart. The delivery comes from practice. Acting, always acting – remember?

Sometimes being a college football coach is like playing a lead in a movie. My dramatic style is simple, I steamroll. I am not passive. I do not want some guy looking up into the sky, and I don't want him looking down at his desk. I want those eyes on me, and if I'm good, that's where they'll be. I will raise my voice, then lower it to a whisper. I will pause to let it sink in. I will be honest. I will be direct. … Motivation is the transference of your heart and soul into your players' minds and bodies. When you do it well, you feel in sync with your team; you can sense its mood. … "Motivation is using what works at the moment." Once in 1978, we were losing to Notre Dame at halftime. Here was my halftime speech, "Gentlemen, it is one thing to be beaten. It is another to be embarrassed,." and I walked out. We won 28-14.

By the way, the notion of fiery halftime speeches is vastly overrated. Oh, I've made a few. By and large, halftime is for adjustments, questions and quick answers. Rarely, will I launch into any motivational lectures at halftime. And I never asked Michigan to 'Win one for the Gipper.' "Verbal, physical, emotional, or comical motivation is a beautiful thing when it works. You must keep up your act, and remember that you are coaching attitude as much as skill. I work on a guy's attitude from the minute he gets here. Encouragement, criticism, screaming, winking, kicking, yelling, nodding, ignoring. It's all part of coaching attitude because attitude equals motivation. … Nothing motivates like your own failure. Nothing!

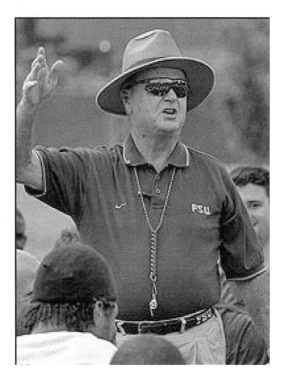

Coach Bobby Bowden, Florida State's Mr. Enthusiasm

Florida State's Coach Bobby Bowden is a firm believer in the power of motivation and enthusiasm. In his book, "<u>The Bowden Way: 50 Years of Leadership Wisdom,</u>" Bowden explains the role of enthusiasm in the game.

Enthusiasm makes a player jump higher, hit harder, and run faster, Bowden writes. The word enthusiasm means, literally, to be filled with divine spirit. Enthusiasm comes from the Greek words en (meaning in) and theos (meaning God). Enthusiastic people possess dynamism and inner drive that seems definitely inspired. They go beyond our average expectations because they are en-thused...filled with the power of divinity.

David, a 40-point underdog to Goliath, was enthused. Moses was enthused. … Enthusiasm can accomplish what every other effort has failed to do. … Football, like any other activity in life, is at least 50 percent emotion. … Complacency is a pervasive phenomenon and a real threat to success. People perform best when they are excited about their work. Nothing scares me on game day like the absence of enthusiasm.

Enthusiasm rises and falls like the tides. It's my job to keep the players as enthusiastic as possible, but I don't fret when the tide goes out. I just turn to my team leaders. Those are the guys I can expect to be enthusiastic when enthusiasm is needed. They'll lead the others in the right direction. … I appeal to their competitive spirit. I appeal to their pride. I appeal to their accomplishments by citing great teams that have played in prior years. I use negative reinforcements when appropriate. …

During my entire coaching career, I've looked for little ways to keep coaches and players motivated to do their best. Motivated people are tough to beat. Morale is different from enthusiasm. Enthusiasm is more of an occasional phenomenon. Some people are enthusiastic almost all of the time. But most people need to be pumped up. Fiery speeches, inspiring stories, direct challenges and satisfying rewards are the stuff used to generate enthusiasm. Morale is more of a day-in and day-out phenomenon.

If team morale is good all week, our players will be amply prepared and motivated for the game on Saturday. But if morale is sagging, my coaches and I must find ways to pump them up and generate some enthusiasm.

Marv Goux, Assistant Coach USC Trojans

The internet is a great source of stories about football. One great story we found tells about a fire breathing coach named, Marv Goux (1933-2002). Goux was an assistant coach of the USC Trojans for 26 years. He was known as a phenomenal motivator with a national reputation. According to tributes, he was the embodiment of Trojan spirit. This quote illustrates his intensity:

"We're going to kick ass and take names! Burn their barns! Pillage the town! Hide the women and children! We're the Men of Troy! We'll take no prisoners! Get one of them before they get you! The best trophy you can win isn't the one on the mantel in your living room or the plaque on the wall in your den. The best trophies are your scars. Those are the ones you'll remember because you'll carry them with you forever."

In the year before Goux's death, former USC offensive lineman Mike Lamb, became a host of a national college football show on Fox Sports Radio. He wrote this regarding the impending USC-Notre Dame match-up in South Bend, Ind, "Big Man on Big Man!" Coach Goux would yell. "You've got to be able to make that play if you're going to beat Notre Dame!" "Beat Notre Dame?!" "These are the games that you remember the rest of your life!" extolled the distinguished young head coach in a dank, cold and not accidentally cramped locker room. It was exactly how you had pictured it, and then again not at all. It seemed almost medieval in its scope. Minuscule cramped quarters where you had to lean your bare skin against cold, wet, yellow brick walls that (Knute) Rockne himself had designed.

You knew the psychological effect that he was aiming for in this marvelously economical layout. But you just had to laugh as you looked at the assembling armada around the room. The walls reverberated with the coaching staff's last few words. It was unusual because this was not a group that lent itself to loud oratory.

You remember the little things, like trying to stretch out your jersey to get it around oversized shoulder pads. Every pull or tug was met with an equal push from your locker mates. Squeezed between Roy Foster's massive legs and arms and Don Mosebar's towering presence, it seemed like rush hour on the C train going into Grand Central Station. Even though he had been thrust upon a national television audience with a game-winning touchdown grab against Oklahoma (his only one, I might add), an engineering student who moonlighted as a tight end was only too happy to provide the correct angle and coordinates at which one could get dressed in such sparse confines. That was the thing about Fred Cornwell. That was the thing about all of these guys. They never let it go to their head. But then again, how could you with the guys you were surrounded by?

In the fourth quarter, Chip Banks hit Greg Bell in the backfield for a loss of two and the crowd let out a deflating groan. Number 51 didn't just hit you to tackle you. He delivered the kind of hit that made you want to go lie down and watch cartoons on Saturday rather than play college football. I can recall the rest of the Irish offense turning away. I thought how the late afternoon clouds made the blue in their jerseys seem even darker, and now mirrored the mood of the home crowd.

The proud fans that had finally come to grips with the reality that Bob Crable knew an hour earlier. It's amazing how right the head coach had been on that cool fall day in Indiana. I can still see his graying temples, the black shiny coach's shoes. The well-worn jacket with the bright gold "Southern Cal" stitched on his coat just above his heart. Those were the days that you never forgot. The grass was dark green and smelled fresh and dewy. The leaves had turned. It felt like it was going to snow that night. It does always comes down to one defining and pivotal moment."

* * *

COACH'S WORDS OF INSPIRATION, MOTIVATION AND WISDOM

The following represent a treasury of favorite quotes submitted from Halftime Book Project contributing coaches. In addition, also included are some powerfully inspiring quotes gleaned from various sources. With eyes closed and a little imagination one can take an imaginary trip to a locker room halftime location and hear the coach rattle off one of these motivational and inspirational pearls of wisdom.

GREG SCHIANO, COACH, RUTGERS

A favorite quote of mine: "This program will be built on a rock foundation. It will take longer than a building on stilts, but when it is built, it will be built forever. Our foundation will be built on "trust." This quote is important to me because our program, starting with our recruiting and the attitude of our players continues to move forward in a positive direction.

MIKE MARTZ, ASSISTANT COACH, DETROIT LIONS

A favorite quote: "Give of yourself completely; ask nothing in return and excellence will be yours." This is the motto of our team. It emphasizes an unselfish giving with excellence as our goal. An illustration of this I can recall: In the fourth quarter of the last game of the 1995 season, Isaac Bruce had a chance to be the all time NFL single season reception and yards leader. He needed just a few catches. The Rams were losing by 3 TD's with 5 minutes left. Isaac refused to go in the game to get the record. He said the record had no meaning to him in a losing situation. His emphasis was not on himself, but on winning and achieving excellence. He taught us all a lesson."

KEN HATFIELD, FORMER COACH,
RICE UNIVERSITY

My favorite quote is from the Bible: "Do you not know that in a race all runners compete, but only one receives the prize. So run that you may obtain it." This is from 1 Corinthians 9:25-25. Football is about one play at a time. If you give your BEST on any particular play-you can be a champion, even if the score is against you. Five runners run, one wins, all can be champions if they gave it all they had."

TOM COUGHLIN, FORMER HEAD COACH, JACKSONVILLE JAGUARS

Here are two of my favorite quotes: "If a man has talent and does not use it, he has failed. If he has a talent and uses only half of it, he has partly failed. If he has a talent and learns somehow to use the whole of it, he has gloriously succeeded ". These are the words of Thomas Wolfe.

* * *

The second quote: "The only difference between those who fail and those who succeed lies in the difference in their habits." These are the words of Robert Fraley. An application of the quotes is illustrated by this story: At our Saturday night team meeting I expressed these quotes to the team. As I stood at the locker room door the next day as our players were ready to take the field, I told our players to take a "ticket" from me as they passed by. I told them that I would collect the tickets at game's end. The players understood the warrior mentality and the kind of effort that is necessary for us to win on that particular Sunday in Pittsburgh. After the game, we gathered in the locker room to celebrate our hard fought victory, It was time for me to collect the tickets!"

FISHER DEBERRY, COACH, AIR FORCE

"My favorite quote is Psalms 118: 24, "This is the day the Lord hath made. Let's rejoice and be glad in it." It is the motivational edge I try to approach each day with. I am so thankful for the opportunity to be a coach. I do hope I can have a positive influence upon those who have been entrusted to us. The attitude that we approach each day and each task with has a lot to do with whether we'll be successful or not.

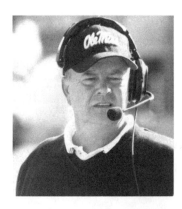

DAVID CUTCLIFFE, ASSISTANT COACH,
UNIVERSITY OF TENNESSEE

One of my favorite quotes is: "No excuses! No regrets!" Prior to my first year at Ole Miss we heard many reasons (Excuses) why something couldn't be done. After listening to everyone and reviewing where we were as a program I told everybody, "thank you for the input, but for then on we would not have any more excuses about our future growth." I made it clear, live your life without regrets! Be Proactive! Get the excuses for failure out of your life

DAVE WANNSTEDT, COACH,
UNIVERSITY OF PITTSBURGH
Former Coach Miami Dolphins, Chicago Bears

I believe that we should, pray like it all depends on God! And work like it all depends on you! God has given each one of us the ability and opportunity with the right effort and attitude we can be successful.

URBAN MEYER, COACH, UNIVERSITY OF FLORIDA

Here are a few of my favorite quotes, "If what you want in the future is different than what you now, you have to change what you are doing!" The difference between winning and losing is extremely fragile. However, not by accident. There is no such thing as luck. John Wooden says, "Do not treat players all the same, treat them how they deserve to be treated."

I took over a program (Bowling Green) that had six consecutive losing seasons. A group of 14 seniors convinced me after our first meeting that they would do whatever it took to have a winning season. We changed everything in 2001: the locker room, uniforms, off season program. The senior class went on to win 8 games (including 3 BCS Conference schools) in the top turnaround season in Division 1A.

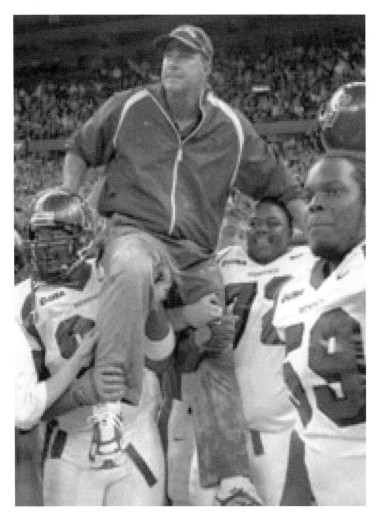

TOMMY WEST, COACH, UNVERSITY OF MEMPHIS

A favorite quote of mine is: "Tough times never last, tough people do!" I believe that every person is going to have adversity in his or her life, whether it is personal or professional. This quote about toughness is very true and I have always kept it close. It is always calm after the storm. These words help me to stand up for what I believe during tough times.

"Nobody who ever gave his best regretted it."
George Halas— Photo Courtesy of the Chicago Bears

Tales From the Chicago Bears Sidelines contains many
good Papa Bear George Halas stories. One story centers on
Hall of Famer, George Connor. Connor was kicked in the head
by a Packer and needed stitches in his chin at halftime. He
went into the boiler room of Lambeau Field, then called City
Stadium, to have the cut stitched up. When he was finished,
he was a little late for the second half and the stadium gates
were padlocked. Connor yelled to some Chicago Bear fans in
the stadium. They came down and soon got into a fight with
stadium people to get the gate open. Finally, Connor ran into
the stadium, but the Bears were on the other side of the field.
At this time play was proceeding. Connor had to wait for a
timeout to run across to their side. "Where have you been?"
Halas yelled. "You're late. That'll cost you $50."

* * *

QUOTABLE SOURCES OF LOCKER ROOM
INSPIRATIONAL WISDOM

Many of us have collected favorite quotes that we find inspirational. In the final chapter we offer a good sampling of favorite quotes from many sources. Any one of them could prove to be a great theme for a memorable halftime motivational pep talk.

Halftime is a fascinating adventure that plays out each game in a unique way. Many secrets of halftime locker rooms are locked up forever. In this book you have had a glimpse of this fascinating part of the game that captivates the interest of so many.

The following are all from the legendary *Vince Lombardi:*

"Coaches who can outline plays on a blackboard are a dime a dozen. The ones who win get inside their players and motivate."

"The price of success is hard work, dedication to the job at hand, and the determination that whether we win or lose, we have applied the best of ourselves to the task at hand."

"The difference between a successful person and others is not a lack of strength, not a lack of knowledge, but rather in a lack of will."

"Winning is not a sometime thing; it's an all time thing. You don't win once in a while, you don't do things right once in a while, you do them right all the time. Winning is habit. Unfortunately, so is losing."

"Leaders aren't born, they are made. And they are made just like anything else, through hard work. And that's the price we'll have to pay to achieve that goal, or any goal."

"Winning is a habit. Unfortunately, so is losing."

"The dictionary is the only place success comes before work. Hard work is the price we must all pay for success"

"I firmly believe that any man's finest hour, the greatest fulfillment of all that he holds dear, is that moment when he has worked his heart out in a good cause and lies exhausted on the field of battle - victorious."

"Football is like life — it requires perseverance, self-denial, hard work, sacrifice, dedication and respect for authority"

"We didn't lose the game; we just ran out of time."

"The hurt is in the mind. No one is really ever hurt"

* * *

"What I have learned in my years as a competitive wheelchair athlete is this: what separates a winner from the rest of the pack is not raw talent or physical ability; instead, it is the drive and dedication to work hard every single day, and the heart to go after your dream, no matter how unattainable others think it is."

Linda Mastandrea

"I do not believe in failure—only results! If I can change what I do, I can always get a different result. Some of the greatest miracles of my life have not come by grand events—but rather by the little things I have chosen to do...every day."

Art Berg

"Failure is not fatal; failing to change will be."

"Sports do not build character. They reveal it."

John Wooden

"Before you can win a game, you have to not lose it."

Chuck Noll, former coach, Pittsburgh Steelers

"Knowing is not enough, you must apply. Willing is not enough, you must do."

"Preparation and Execution are the Keys to Victory and Success"

Douglas McArthur

"The country is full of good coaches. What it takes to win is a bunch of interested players."

Don Coryell, former coach, San Diego Chargers

"The pessimist complains about the wind. The optimist expects it to change. The leader adjusts the sails."

John Maxwell

"Coming together is a beginning; keeping together is progress; working together is success."

Henry Ford

"We are what we repeatedly do. Excellence then, is not an act, but a habit"

Aristotle

"Nothing great was ever achieved without enthusiasm."

Henry David Thoreau

"The miracle, or the power, that elevates the few is to be found in their industry, application, and perseverance under the prompting of a brave, determined spirit."

Mark Twain

"Permanence, perseverance and persistence in spite of all obstacles, discouragement, and impossibilities: It is this that in all things distinguishes the strong soul from the weak."

Thomas Carlyle

"If I was given eight hours to chop down a tree. I would spend seven hours sharpening my ax"

"I do the best I know how, the very best I can; and I mean to keep on doing it to the end. If the end brings me out all right, what is said against me will not amount to anything. If the end brings me out all wrong, ten angels swearing I was right would make no difference"

Abraham Lincoln

"To find the unlimited scope of human possibility, look within yourself."

Jim Valvano

Never tell people how to do things. Tell them what to do and they will surprise you with their ingenuity.

George S. Patton

"What lies behind us and what lies before us are tiny matters compared to what lies within us."

Ralph Waldo Emerson

"There are no great people in this world, only great challenges which ordinary people rise to meet."

William Frederick Halsy, Jr.

"Enthusiasm is that secret and harmonious spirit which hovers over the production of genius."

Isaac Disraeli

"Flaming enthusiasm backed by horse sense and persistence, is the quality that most frequently makes for success."

Dale Carnegie

"When one door closes another door opens; but we so often look so long and so regretfully upon the closed door, that we do not see the ones which open for us."

"No pessimist ever discovered the secret of the stars, or sailed to an uncharted land, or opened a new doorway for the human spirit."

"Optimism is the faith that leads to achievement. Nothing can be done without hope and confidence."

Helen Keller

"They can not take away our self respect if we do not give it to them."

Mahatma Gandhi

"Whether you think you can or think you can't, you are right."

Henry Ford

"Setting a goal is not the main thing. It is deciding how you will go about achieving it and staying with that plan." Tom Landry

"The will to win is important, but the will to prepare is vital."

Joe Paterno

"It's not the size of the dog in the fight, but the size of the fight in the dog."

Archie Griffin

"Before you can win, you have to believe you are worthy."

Mike Ditka

"You gain strength, courage and confidence by every experience in which you stop to look fear in the face."

Eleanor Roosevelt

"The capacity for hope is the most significant fact of life. It provides human beings with a sense of destination and the energy to get started."

Norman Cousins

"There are only two ways to live your life. One is as though nothing is a miracle. The other is as if everything is."

Albert Einstein

"The best way to cheer yourself up is to cheer everybody else up."

Mark Twain

"Challenges are what make life interesting; overcoming them is what makes life meaningful."

Joshua J. Marine

"A rock pile ceases to be a rock pile the moment a single man contemplates it, bearing within him the image of a cathedral."

Antoine de Saint-Exupéry

"Most of the important things in the world have been accomplished by people who have kept on trying when there seemed to be no hope at all."

Dale Carnegie

"In the long run, men hit only what they aim at. Therefore, they had better aim at something high."

Henry David Thoreau

"Far better it is to dare mighty things to win glorious triumphs, even though checkered with failure, than to take rank with those poor spirits who neither enjoy much nor suffer much, because they live in the gray twilight that know not victory or defeat."

Theodore Roosevelt

"A man is not finished when he is defeated. He is finished when he quits."

Richard Nixon

"If one advances confidently in the direction of his dreams, and endeavors to live the life which he has imagined, he will meet with a success unexpected in common hours."

Henry David Thoreau

"The individual activity of one man with backbone will do more than a thousand men with a mere wishbone."

William Boetcker

"It's not my job to motivate players. They bring extraordinary motivation to our program. It's my job not to de-motivate them."

"Motivation is simple. You eliminate those who are not motivated."

"Almost everything that happens to us - good or bad- is a result of the decisions we make; we choose to be happy or sad, believe or doubt, pray or curse, help or heal, work or loaf, succeed or fail."

"Ability is what you're capable of doing... Motivation determines what you do... Attitude determines how well you do it.

"The answer to three questions will determine your success or failure.
1. Can people trust me to do my best?.
2. Am I committed to the task in hand?.
3. Do I care about other people and show it?

If the answers to all three questions are yes, there is no way you can fail."

"How you respond to the challenge in the second half will determine what you become after the game, whether you are a winner or a loser"

Lou Holtz

"The ones who want to achieve and win championships motivate themselves."

How you respond to the challenge in the second half will determine what you become after the game, whether you are a winner or a loser."

"Ability is what you're capable of doing. Motivation determines what you do. Attitude determines how well you do it."

"If you're bored with life, you don't get up every morning with a burning desire to do things, you don't have enough goals."

Mike Ditka

"If you don't invest very much, then defeat doesn't hurt very much and winning is not very exciting"

Dick Vermeil

"Accept the challenges, so that you may feel the exhilaration of victory"

Patton

"Paralyze resistance with persistence"

Woody Hayes

"Nothing in the world can take the place of persistence. Talent will not; nothing is more common than unsuccessful men with talent. Genius will not; unrewarded genius is almost a proverb. Education will not; the world is full of educated derelicts. Persistence and determination alone are omnipotent. The slogan 'Press On' has solved and always will solve the problems of the human race."

Calvin Coolidge

In business, sports, and life — these principles apply. There is no easy shortcut to success. Success is made from planning, hard work, dedication, and determination, helping others, some luck and a good relationship with God.

"People who are in it for their own good are individualists. They don't share the same heartbeat that makes a team so great. A great unit, whether it be football or any organization, shares the same heartbeat."

"I have always tried to teach my players to be fighters. When I say that, I don't mean put up your dukes and get in a fistfight over something. I'm talking about facing adversity in your life. There is not a person alive who isn't going to have some awfully bad days in their lives. I tell my players that what I mean by fighting is when your house burns down, and your wife runs off with the drummer, and you've lost your job and all the odds are against you. What are you going to do?

Most people just lay down and quit. Well, I want my people to fight back."

Paul "Bear" Bryant

REFERENCES

David Maraniss, When Pride Still Mattered-A Life of Vice Lombardi. (New York: Touchstone Books, 1999.)

Bill Chastain, The Steve Spurrier Story: From Heisman to Head Ball Coach. (Lanham, Maryland, Taylor Trade Publishing, 2002)

Dick Butkus and Pat Smith, Butkus-Flesh and Blood: How I Played the Game. (New York: Doubleday, 1997)

Gene Schoor, Football's Greatest Coach: Vince Lombardi, New York: Doubleday, 1974)
Lou Holtz, Winning Every Day. (New York: HarperCollins Books, 1999)

American Football Coaches Association, The Football Coaching Bible, (Champaign, Illinois: Human Kinetics, 2002)

American Football Coaches Association, Football Coaching Strategies, (Champaign, Illinois: Human Kinetics, 1995)

Gary Barnett with Vahe Gregorian, High Hopes: Taking the Purple to Pasadena. (NY. Warner Books, 1996)

John Madden with Dave Anderson, One Knee Equals Two Feet (And Everything Else You Need To Know About Football), (NY, Jove Books. 1986)

Hank Nuwer, Strategies of the Great Football Coaches, (New York: Franklin Watts, 1988)

Bob and Brian Griese with Jim Denny, Undefeated, (Nashville: Thomas Nelson, 2000)

Billy Packer with Roland Lazenby, Why We Win-Great American Coaches Offer Their Strategies for Success in Sports and Life, (Chicago: Masters Press, 1999)

John Wiebusch (Ed), Lombardi, (Chicago: Triumph Books, 1997)

Phil Barber and Ray Didinger, Football America-Celebrating Out National Passion, (Atlanta: Turner Publishing, Inc.,1996)

Mike Shanahan with Adam Schefter, Think Like a Champion, (New York: HarperCollins, 2000)

Bo Schembechler and Mitch Albom, Bo: Life, Laughs, and Lessons of a College Football Legend, (New York: Warner Books, 1989.)

Nick Saban with Sam King, Tiger Turnaround-LSU's Return to Football Glory, (Chicago: Triumph Books, 2002)

Joe Hoppel, Mike Nahrstedt, Steve Zesch,(Ed) (The Sporting News College Football's Twenty-Five Greatest Teams, St. Louis: The Sporting News, 1988)

Bill Lyon, When the Clock Runs Out-20 NFL Greats Share Their Stories of Hardship and Triumph, (Chicago: Triumph Books, 1999)

Sam Brown and Sam Carchidi, Miracle in the Making, The Adam Taliaferro Story, (Chicago: Triumph Books, 2001.)

Grant Teaff with Louis and Kay Moore, Winning: It's How You Play the Game. (Waco: Word Books, 1985.)

Monte Carpenter, Quotable Lou, (Nashville: Towle House Publishing, 2002)

Bobby Bowden, and family, Winning's Only Part of the Game, (New York: Warner Books, 1996.)

Kurt Warner with Michael Silver, All Things Possible, (New York: HarperCollins, 2000.)

Brian D. Bero, Beyond Success, (New York: Perigee Books, 1997).

Tom Landry with Gregg Lewis, Tom Landry: An Autobiography, (New York: HarperCollins Publishers, 1990.)

Lorne A. Adrian ed, The Most Important Thing I know About the Spirit of Sport, (New York: William Morrow and Co., 1999.)

Richard Whittingham, Bears in their Own Words, (Chicago: Contemporary Books, 1991)

Brian Billick, Competitive Leadership: Twelve Principles for Success, (Chicago: Triumph Books, 2001)

Don Shula and Ken Blanchard, Everyone's a Coach-You Can Inspire Anyone to be a Winner, (New York: Harper Business, 1995).

Bobby Bowden with Steve Bowden, The Bowden Way, 50 years of Leadership Wisdom, (Atlanta: Longstreet Press, 2001.)

Dan Reeves with Dick Connor, Reeves: An Autobiography, (Chicago: Bonus Books, 1988.)

Tom Osborne, Faith in the Game, (New York: Broadway Books, 1999).

Tim Green, The Dark Side of the Game: My Life in the NFL, (New York: Warner Books, 1996.)

Steve Singular and Moose Krause, Notre Dame's Greatest Coaches, (New York: Pocket Books, 1993)

John Wiebusch, ed., The NFL Super Bowl Companion, (Chicago: Triumph Books, 2002)

Ray Didinger ed., Game Plans for Success-Winning Strategies for Business and Life From 10 Top NFL Coaches, (Boston Little, Brown and Company)

APPENDICES

The following pages were part of a six page packet mailed on January 1, 2003 to over 300 coaches in the NFL, and Division 1 college programs. Responses came back in many forms, email, fax, phone messages and mail.

HALF TIME
CONTRIBUTOR'S IDEA GENERATOR

Consider the Following to Get the Creative Juices Flowing

How do you approach half time? Rest? Re-focus? Set new strategy? Make adjustments? Correct?

Do you typically talk individually to players? Talk to the whole group?

Is the normal pattern high emotion? Motivation? Inspiration? Instruction? Assignments?

What's the typical agenda and time frame? What's the experience like once the locker room door is closed?

Are there traditional rules and expectations for players during half-time?

The best analogy I can make about half time, is that this time is like:

The feeling I usually have after leaving the locker room at half time is:

THE
HALF TIME
PROJECT AS TOLD BY COACHING GREATS FROM THE NCAA AND NFL

Rob Komosa

Rocky Cla

Dear Coach:

We are eager to share with you news of an exciting and important project. You are cordially invited to join efforts to assist two Chicago area paralyzed high school football players, **Rocky Clark** and **Rob Komosa**, and their families.

We are inviting celebrated NFL and NCAA coaches to participate in the compilation of significant half-time moments from their careers. *Your own contribution* could take the form of an *anecdote; a memorable event; a humorous incident; a historic circumstance; an inspiring/motivating talk* or some other special moment. These contributions will be compiled into a book to share with readers nationwide as an inspiration to everyone who is facing adversity in their lives.

Half-time conversations are often very private moments, however, we also realize that football fans are fascinated with how that special football spirit and motivation is transformed into heightened on-field performance. We hope to reveal an "inside look" at how coaches and players prepare for the second half of a contest. We earnestly believe this book can make an important contribution to the history of the game.

Proceeds of this book will go towards supporting and motivating young quadriplegic athletes. We have been working diligently to inspire them as they strive to overcome their obstacles. With your help, we will be able to send a half-time message of hope and optimism that will carry them enthusiastically into the second half of their lives.

Rocky Clark and Rob Komosa's courageous personal stories are described in this mailing. Additional pages describe how easy it is for you to personally contribute to this project. Enclosed is a sample of the working prototype. We earnestly hope you will take time from your busy schedule and generously share a special moment with America. *We ask that you submit your half-time wisdom with us by February 15, 2003*, so that our book will be ready for the fall season of 2003. In order to begin working on the details of the project, an addressed postcard is enclosed to let us know if you are willing to participate. In the event you have any questions, please contact one of the project coordinators who will be most happy to assist you.

Sincerely,

Randy Walker,
Coach, NU

Dick Jauron
Coach, Chicago Bears

Project Coordinator: Dr. Don Grossnickle
1253 S. Walnut Ave.
Arlington Heights, IL 60005
phone: (847)956-7432
fax: (630)628-0177
email: dgrossnick@aol.com